ALMOST

Andrew L Dodds

MINERVA PRESS
LONDON
MIAMI RIO DE JANEIRO DELHI

ALMOST
Copyright © Andrew L Dodds 2001

All Rights Reserved

No part of this book may be reproduced in any form
by photocopying or by any electronic or mechanical means,
including information storage or retrieval systems,
without permission in writing from both the copyright
owner and the publisher of this book.

ISBN 0 75411 532 1

First Published 2001 by
MINERVA PRESS
315–317 Regent Street
London W1B 2HS

Printed in Great Britain for Minerva Press

ALMOST

Extract from *Muirkirk, A Miscellany*, by Tom Findlay reproduced with kind permission of his wife.

Foreword

Andrew Lynn Dodds was born in Muirkirk, Ayrshire on 22 August 1926. He was the fourth son of James Dodds, a miner, and Elizabeth Flanagan. There was another member of the family, a son, who was older than Andrew, Hector McNair. Hector had been adopted by Andrew's parents shortly after their marriage, and was only two months younger than Jim, the oldest member of the family. Three sisters were born after Andrew, increasing the number of children to eight by November 1932. The whole family in age order was as follows:

Father: James,	born 3 September 1900
Mother: Elizabeth,	born 10 September 1902
James,	born 10 November 1921
Hector,	born 22 January 1922
John,	born 13 March 1923
Matthew,	born 13 September 1924
Andrew,	born 22 August 1926
Maisie,	born 3 April 1928
Anna,	born 26 September 1930
Elizabeth (Betty),	born 17 November 1932

Andrew was educated at Muirkirk Higher Grade School but, like his brothers, left at the age of fourteen. His first job as soon as he reached his fourteenth birthday was at Lightshaw Farm where his wage was one pound and ten shillings (£1.50) *a month*, plus board and lodging. That was in the summer of 1940. After about three weeks, working twelve to fourteen hours a day, Andrew got a job at the Kennox Colliery at Glespin, Lanarkshire, where he was paid just over £2 a week for six days' work.

Andrew was not happy working in the pit, and was beginning to regret not taking the advice of his headmaster, Mr Gordon, who had told him to pursue an academic education rather than leave school at fourteen.

In May 1943, an opportunity arose for a job as an engine cleaner in the Motive Power depot in Muirkirk, and after considerable difficulty with the wartime regulations in transferring from one employment to another, he began work as an engine cleaner, later becoming a steam engine fireman.

After only just over six years on the railway, Andrew qualified as a driver. At the age of twenty-three, he was the youngest qualified steam engine driver in Scotland. Twenty-three was the minimum age in those days for being a driver. He just happened to be next in turn to qualify. Tuition was informal; Willie Hamilton, a driver at the depot, was the unofficial instructor. Andrew proved able to pass the rigorous practical examination which took place over two whole days.

Later that same year, he was to become the branch secretary of the Muirkirk branch of the National Union of Railwaymen, the first step on that long journey which *almost* took him to the leadership of a great National Trade Union some thirty-eight years later.

He became a member of the Labour Party around the same time as he became a branch secretary, and was active in the wider Labour Movement, politically and industrially. His activity in the Union broadened and he became an Executive Committee member of the Glasgow and West of Scotland District Council of the Union as well.

Around the end of 1948, Andrew met Margaret Mitchell, the daughter of Robert and Jemima Mitchell of Auchinleck, at the Cumnock Town Hall dances he used to attend with his friends. Andrew and his good friend, George Christie, organised dances in the district for a local dance band, the Modernaires. They attended dances in the valley towns of Galston, Newmilns and Darvel as well as Mauchline, Catrine, Auchinleck, Cumnock and Lugar.

Margaret's father was a railway clerk in Auchinleck, much higher socially in those days than an engine fireman, indeed a pillar of society. Her romance with Andrew blossomed to the point where they married in July 1951, and took up residence in the railway buildings adjoining the engine shed in Muirkirk. Phyllis, the first of their two daughters, was born on 2 October 1953. In the summer of 1954, Andrew was made redundant and decided to move to Hurlford Depot to continue his railway career. They were soon to find accommodation in railway property at Bonnyton Square in Kilmarnock.

Andrew continued his activity in the Union within Hurlford branch, and was made chairman of that branch shortly after arriving in Kilmarnock. A good friend of Andrew's, Bob Banks, a Town Councillor and Provost of Kilmarnock, was encouraging Andrew in local political affairs as well as in the Trade Union Movement, and it was not long before he was contesting Council elections in Kilmarnock, representing the Labour Party.

A second daughter, Alison, was born to Andrew and Margaret on 22 January 1960. By this time Andrew had left the footplate, taking up a position as a clerk in the depot at Hurlford as a means to easing the stomach ulcers he had been suffering from for some years.

Around this time the headquarters of the Union in London were seeking administrative staff, and Andrew applied for one of those positions. This was a few months before Alison's arrival, and it also coincided with Andrew's invitation to fill a vacancy on the Town Council.

All three crises occurred around the same time, causing great headaches about what to do, as he had successfully passed the entrance examination for employment with the Union and had been offered a position. He had also become a Town Councillor, the briefest ever, attending one meeting only early in 1960, in addition to having become a father for the second time.

A book could be written about the events of the first three months of 1960 in the life of Andrew and Margaret Dodds, let alone the thirty-one years that followed that period.

On arrival at Unity House in March 1960, Andrew became Andy and began work in the branch accounts section of the Finance Department. He continued his activity within the Union, and became the Secretary of Harrow and Wealdstone branch for a short period in 1964–65.

He attended evening classes to learn shorthand and typing in order to gain promotion, and passed the necessary standard exam before the end of 1963, being promoted to take charge of the branch accounts section.

It was natural for Andy to become involved in staff affairs, and he was soon a member of the Staff Committee, and became Staff Chairman in 1963, a position he held until 1965.

In 1966, vacancies for two Union Organisers arose, and Andy was nominated by his branch, and many of those in Scotland that he had retained contact with.

To take part in the ballot for Union Organiser, you had to have the requisite number of nominations and length of service in the Union, and sit a two-part examination in the financial affairs of the Union and separately in industrial agreements.

Andy passed the examination at his first attempt, and perhaps more surprisingly was elected to the second of the two vacancies, taking up the position of Road Transport Organiser in October 1966.

In 1967 he was transferred to become the Organiser for London South-East, Kent, Sussex and Surrey, a position he held until being appointed a National Officer in April 1975 at Unity House.

Andy was elected an Assistant General Secretary in December 1981 with one of the highest majorities ever achieved. He took up his final position as Senior Assistant General Secretary in 1987 and in the tradition of most of his predecessors was elected to the Labour Party National Executive each year until he retired in 1991.

Andy was a member of many bodies in the wider industrial movement, such as Industrial Tribunals, Training Boards and the National Dock Labour Board, all government appointments.

There it is, then: almost fifty-one years in the Trade Union Movement, forty-eight in the NUR and its successor, and three in the once great Miners' Union.

Introduction

This autobiography is mainly due to my daughter, Alison, who insisted that she wanted Daniel (my first grandchild) and herself to know more about my background than I was able to tell her about my own parents' background. When I began this work I did not realise how much truth there was in Alison's view. I realised very soon that I knew very little about my father or my mother, in relation to their respective families, how they came to meet or indeed anything else. All I knew was that when I was born on 22 August 1926, there were already four brothers before me, and the eldest was then not even five years old.

Can you imagine this in the context of the second quarter of the twentieth century? Bearing in mind that 2.4 children per family was about the norm twenty-five years later.

I learned as I got older that my four brothers, one of whom was Hector McNair (adopted), were all born in Cambuslang. It was at that time the largest village in Scotland, about six miles or so from the centre of Glasgow. It was a mining and steel-making town where my father had lived with his parents and family.

We later learned that the family whom Mother regarded as her parents in Muirkirk, with a sister and two brothers, were not really her parents at all. How she came to be with them is a complete mystery to the remaining members of the family, my two sisters and my other brother. Mother would surely have loved to have told us before she died in 1963. Apparently, after my birth in Muirkirk, we moved back to Cambuslang, where Maisie was born in April 1928. Some time after that we moved back to Muirkirk again, where Anna was born in 1930 and Betty in 1932. We only know those facts through a study of our respective birth certificates. As children in the 1930s we were kept very much in the dark.

That is not a criticism, because I am sure it was done for the best of reasons, and we were a close family, with a mother who was the nearest to an angel I have ever known. How she coped is beyond description. Although we learned later that in her family, Gran and Granddad Flanagan were not Mother's natural parents, it was my mother who looked after them until they died. How odd it seemed that my mother had been brought up in circumstances similar to Hector's; and for all I know, this could have had some bearing on Hector becoming part of our family. One thing is for sure: like all of us, he worshipped my mother. I am not ashamed to say that Hector and I had as close a relationship as I had with any of my natural brothers.

Sadly he was killed in a pit accident in 1962 at Muirkirk when he was only forty years old.

The nearest I got to learning anything about my father's background was that he was born in Newcastle, Co. Down, Northern Ireland, in September 1900. I never found out when he came to Scotland, although I well remember my Grandmother and Grandfather Dodds, and remember visiting them and staying with them on occasions in Cambuslang.

One of my father's two sisters – Aunt Margaret – was living in the South when I moved to London in 1960. We kept a close relationship with her until she died in Bracknell in 1995, aged ninety-three; but she would not discuss the family in case it revealed to me what age she was. She was a lovely lady, far too good to have been my father's sister. She used to laugh when I told her that. Margaret, Phyllis, Alison and I were all very fond of Aunt Margaret. She always spoke highly of my mother.

It appeared that the toing and froing between Cambuslang and Muirkirk had quite a lot to do with my father being a bit of an agitator as a Union activist in the Miners' Union in those days. Some might say, 'Like father like son'. In fact my brother John was the one who took more after my father as far as agitation was concerned, both as a worker and in the Miners' Union.

I began my Union activity in the National Union of Railwaymen, which was always regarded as much more docile than the Miners' Union. (Arthur Scargill would no doubt agree.)

I am sure that given a more natural development as a family we would have learned all we wanted to about our parents' background, but my father was one of the many miners who often suffered serious accidents at work in the pits. I can remember about three of them, although there were more. The last one was when he and my brother Jim were working at the coal face in late 1939 or early 1940, when his leg was badly smashed. For some reason, when he recovered about a year later, he joined the merchant navy, where he had served as a boy seaman. (The dates are a bit hazy, the facts brutally clear.) The day after my father's last pit accident, Jim joined the air force, deciding that even in wartime he preferred his chances of survival there to those in the pits. Unlike my father, he came through the war unscathed, settled in Scarborough with his wife, Edith (whom he met during the war), and raised a lovely family of three children: Jean, James and Stephen. Until this day they all still live in the North and West Yorkshire area with their respective families.

Brother John settled in Doncaster. Both he and Jim have had sons, thus keeping the Dodds name alive in Yorkshire.

As I have indicated, through our father leaving home at the start of the war to go to sea, we got no chance to discuss anything with him in relation to the earlier years when we were growing up.

The irony of events – as one might expect – was that after less than a year at sea, during which he had been at Gibraltar and in the United States, he got a position on a coaster in Scotland. This eased my mother's anxieties, because in wartime there was no way out of the services once you were in, except in the traditional wooden box. I remember visiting Dad on his ship in Ardrossan harbour some time around early 1942. It was called the SS *Clermiston*, as I later learned.

It was not long after that time that my mother was informed that three of the crew of the *Clermiston* had been ashore when the ship was anchored in the Holy Loch near Dunoon. As they were returning to their ship in a dinghy, it had filled with water, and they were all drowned. My father's body and that of one of his colleagues were found immediately, but the other crew member was not found until about three months after the accident. That happened on 30 June 1942, when I was about two months short of my sixteenth birthday, and my mother about three months short of her fortieth birthday.

My adult life was only beginning, and that of my three young sisters had not even begun. In fact my mother, still in her thirties, was facing life with a family of eight and no husband. I suppose that, as it was wartime and the oldest five were already working, including me, at least financially things might have been worse. What a cruel world I seemed to be entering as an adolescent, and what hardships my mother was yet to endure.

Chapter One

When Anna was born in 1930 there were by then seven children in the family, including Hector, and we lived in a two-apartment miner's house in a single-storey row of about fifty-six houses, one or two of which had three apartments.

Our house was Number 26, Springhill Terrace, and had three bed recesses – two in the living room and one in the bedroom. None of the rooms were bigger than 12' x 10', and they were lit by gas and heated with a large open fire where most of the cooking was also done. Water was brought from a pump in the roadway outside the house, and we shared a dry outside lavatory with about four other families.

As far as I can recall, around 1930 or '31, after Anna was born, Jim, Hector and John slept in the bed in the bedroom, while Maisie slept at the bottom of the living-room bed that Matt and I slept in. Mother and Father slept in the other bed in the living room. This arrangement was not at all uncommon, as most families were large in number, the very largest having an extra room, but that was not the case in more than about four houses out of the fifty-six in the row. It was probably when Betty was born in November 1932 that Jim went to live with Grandfather and Grandma Flanagan in the Smallburn, which was on the other side of the village.

The village was in two parts: the miners' rows named the Southside, or locally, 'O'er the Water'; and about one half to three-quarters of a mile away was what we called the 'Toon'.

The story gets complicated around this point because, as I explained earlier, our toing and froing between Muirkirk and Cambuslang, according to the address of my birth, indicates I was born in the Kames Row which actually backed on to the Springhill Row, where I mainly remember living. The two rows of houses referred to were separated by a broad strip of grass, maybe about thirty feet wide.

There was not meant to be any direct access or exit to this from the houses, but some of us used the window to get in and out. Nearly all the houses had only a dirt track in front of them, although two of the later-built rows, Springhill and Park Terrace (locally known as the 'Honeymoon Row' because a lot of newly-weds took up residence in it), had a pavement in front of the row. At the front of the houses there were brick-built blocks containing the wash-houses, coal cellars and lavatories. Each block, containing one wash-house and about two lavatories, served about six families. Each family had the use of the wash-house for one day each week. I can well remember lighting the boiler fire for my mother before going to school, and finding her still in the wash-house when I came home from school about seven hours later. As I recall, we didn't have very many clothes, maybe one change each, which, if you multiply by seven and add in some bed sheets and towels, probably meant enough to keep Mother busy. I also recall Mother did our granny's washing because our Matt and I often collected it on the way home from school, and returned it when it was all done a day or two later.

It must have been around 1934 or '35 when they installed outside lavatories with water cisterns, one between two families (like being in heaven), and took cold water into each house with a sink (paradise). This was really a gigantic step forward from what we had been used to. But there was no more space indoors for beds, and when Betty had arrived in November 1932 she should have been named Jesus, because, just as his parents found in Bethlehem, there was no room for Betty in our house either. In her early days she lived with our next-door neighbour.

The seven to eight years that I can remember in the Springhill Row, as we called it, were very happy times, even though we must have been very poor. As I have said earlier, Dad was out of work often in that period, but my mum was such a good provider that I don't recall going hungry very often.

Mum said in fact we were better off when Dad wasn't working, as long as he hadn't been injured, because he would go poaching for hares and rabbits, and occasionally would bring us a chicken or an old hen. We never asked where he got them. He also 'acquired' plenty of potatoes, turnips, cabbage, logs and coal for heating and cooking.

Our mother would from time to time put new wallpaper on and do a bit of painting as well. She knitted continually for us all, jumpers, socks and stockings, often with wool rippled out of older garments, sometimes given by neighbours. Mother had a Singer sewing machine, an old treadle type, and it was a godsend, because with it she made nearly all the girls' clothes, school pinafores and skirts, and many a time she made trousers for us boys. All the cloth in those garments came again from old adult garments, with the stitching unpicked, and where it was serge cloth she was able to use the reverse or unworn side. When the woollen garments were no longer fit to be unravelled, we would help her cut them into strips, and she would use a piece of canvas Father 'acquired' at the pit, where it was used as what they called 'screen cloth', and Mum would draw a flowery pattern on the canvas, and make a new hearthrug. We usually only had a rug by the door, and one at the hearth. To sit on a new hearthrug at New Year was regarded as one of the luxuries of the time. Sometimes the canvas used would be a sugar bag obtained from the local Co-op. Most mothers also made a coarse apron – for scrubbing the floor or for the wash-house – out of a sugar bag.

We had a vegetable garden that we made use of, which helped to make up the plentiful supply of vegetables we had in the season. We all learned how to improvise during those times.

Even though life in regard to material things appeared hard, my memories of those times were generally happy ones. Friends, neighbours and relatives nearly all shared the same experiences. My clearest memories are from the time I began school, which would be around August 1931. My first teacher was a Miss Benny; she was not very old, but quite stern. I remember that day very vividly because I wet myself in the classroom, and she made me sit on the big hot pipes until I dried. Because of that memory of the warm pipes it may well have been after Christmas when I started school in January 1932.

Muirkirk was a fairly big village in those days. The population of around five thousand was divided between the two parts of the village. The Southside (O'er the Water), where all the miners' rows were, had around two thousand a population. All the property in that part of the village was owned by the colliery company, Baird & Dalmellington, with the exception of one double-storey building which belonged to the railway company, London, Midland and Scottish Railway. That property is where I took up residence when I got married in 1951, but more about that later.

The colliery company also owned a store, mainly selling groceries and booze, known as the 'Old Store' to distinguish it from the Co-operative, which sold everything. The 'Old Store' was situated halfway between the two parts of the village adjoining the company offices. In earlier times there had been furnaces in the village, producing iron from pig-iron brought from Spain. In fact there was at least one Spanish family in the village, who had settled there in connection with that industry.

I continued to live in the Springhill Row with my brothers and sisters until August 1939. As I said earlier, when Betty arrived in 1932 and was past the baby stage, she mainly lived with our next-door neighbours. That and the fact that Jim continued to live with our grandparents in the Smallburn gave two extra bed spaces. There were only a few council houses in the Town part of the village, but I remember some being built early in the 1930s, maybe about 1933, adjoining the graveyard.

These were used to rehouse a number of the families from the Smallburn, and our grandparents were allocated one of them. I don't know what criteria they used for allocating council houses, but it was great for Granny and Grandpa – and for our Jim who lived with them – to move into a home with two bedrooms and a living room, as well as a bathroom and kitchen with hot and cold water. There was also a garden separated from the cemetery only by an eight-foot-high wall. Granny used to tell Grandpa, 'You needn't think I'll be eating anything oot o' that garden!'

The seven other children in our family and Mum and Dad, as I have said, continued life in the Rows, but at least we could now go to Granny's for a bath.

Grandpa didn't live long on the wrong side of the cemetery.

He died shortly after moving, and instead of us joining Granny, Mother got her a house in Honeymoon Row to be near her. Granny died not long after Granddad, in about 1936, I think.

Meanwhile, Jim had started work in a pit in Lanarkshire, seven miles from our village, the same pit where I was to get a job when I was fourteen in 1940. The pit was locally known as 'Cornycoup'; it was in fact Kennox Colliery, but known after the local 'big house', Carmacoup House. Jim later left that pit and went to work in the Muirkirk pit, the 'Kames', where Hector was already working, there being only two months' difference in their ages. They were joined by John, although I am not sure whether that was immediately when they left school at fourteen. Right up until the war began in September 1939, work was scarce, as it was all through the Depression years of the thirties. Jim's wages went to Granny's house as far as I was aware, but when Hector started work, and then later John, we were beginning to be an affluent family. I am sure Mother didn't notice it, as if there was any extra, my father could make use of more than his share of it. Jim showed signs of having a good brain at school, and at the eleven-plus stage began a preliminary academic course; but as the eldest of a big family, he was expected to start earning as soon as possible, and to his credit he did just that.

I am sure that he had a very happy life with his lovely wife, Edith, his daughter, Jean, and sons, James and Stephen, and latterly his grandchildren, around him.

Those seven or eight years from about 1930–31 until we moved to the Town in August 1939 were very happy, even if life seemed harsh. I said before, all my pals were in much the same boat, and while there may have been smaller families, they seemed to help out those of us from larger families. I have vivid memories of the young men coming from the pit every day around 4 p.m. – those who were working – and playing football almost continually until it was dark. The teams got bigger and bigger and when they reached about fifteen a side another game would start. Very often on a Friday, pay day, they would contribute a few coppers each and send one of us to the Town to buy a new ball for about 2s 6d – 12½p in today's money. Whoever went was sure to get 2d or 3d or whatever amount was over the cost of the ball to keep. That particular errand was very much in demand on a Friday, as 3d was quite a lot of money.

We seemed to have so many activities to keep us occupied that there never seemed a dull moment in those years. Football was a major sport in all the mining villages, and indeed every village had really good schoolboy teams. There was no school team better in the district than Muirkirk, and in fact quite a number of the team from around the 1934–35–36 period went on to become professionals. The standard was so good at that time that I can remember special trains going to some of the games in neighbouring villages, never further than about fourteen miles away.

The reason my memory is so vivid on this matter is that I knew a young man of about my brother Jim's age, nearly five years older than me, named Adam Black. Adam, who lived near my granny in Honeymoon Row, was crippled and confined to a type of wheelchair which he had to lie in like a bed. Adam was befriended by many in the village, but I took him out a lot in his chair. He was a very popular chap in the village, and I never knew the cause of his disability. I can remember when he could once walk with sticks and leg splints, but shortly after he left school he became totally disabled. Like many disabled people he had a great spirit.

One particular villager used to pay for Adam and me on the special trains to the school football matches. The benefactor was Geordie Stevens, a local insurance man. He was a member of a family who produced one of the finest mining engineers in the country, Bob Stevens, and I think, the eminent cancer surgeon, Tom (later Sir Tom) Symington was their nephew.

I spent many happy days taking Adam out and about, particularly during our school holidays. He was a very popular fellow with nearly everybody in the village, and I am sure I benefited from Adam's popularity.

I mentioned earlier about brother Jim's educational ability, and it appears that some of it had rubbed off on to me. When we took the eleven-plus exam in those days, those who appeared to the headmaster, Mr Gordon, to be academic material were creamed off and spent a period of each day in his personal charge being prepared for such a course. Your parents had to give their written authority for the actual academic course to begin. My brother Matt had been giving me advice contrary to the headmaster, telling me how miserable I would be studying Latin, French and other academic subjects when he and the rest of our friends would be enjoying themselves, playing football, swimming, bird-nesting and all the other glorious pursuits we indulged in.

The time came when Mr Gordon sent me home early one lunchtime to have this 'form of consent' signed. Father was in bed sleeping, being on night shift. Mother already knew I was opposed to going to the higher-grade classes (as they were referred to), and after asking me if that was still my view, which I said it was, she said there seemed no point in waking Dad. I returned to school with the unsigned form and a cold reception from the headmaster. There were no parent–teacher organisations in those days, and no thought apparently given to the headmaster seeing one or other of my parents to explain the possible consequences of their decision.

As circumstances developed, I probably benefited from not following an academic education. It is unlikely that if I had done I would have become a qualified steam train driver after six and a half years on the railway, and everything which that led to in later life. Who knows, maybe I would have become General Secretary of the Union and not just the Deputy. More about that later…

Although I am content in that I had a happy and worthwhile career, it does show how important it is to have parents and the individual children fully involved in their futures.

I am equally content that on this occasion I did not suffer from ignoring the advice of professionals like Mr Gordon, the headmaster, as compared with accepting the advice of brother Matt. I would say that to be on the safe side I would advocate accepting the advice of your headmaster rather than that of your brother. If you had known Matt as well as I did in those days, although we were very close, you would have needed your head examined about accepting any advice he gave. Developments in later life again, as far as Matt was concerned, proved once more that there is more to succeeding in life than paper qualifications. Matt managed to succeed without them too.

It has to be remembered that at this stage in my life, at about eleven years of age, I had completed two-thirds of my formal education. While I appeared to have the capacity for an academic education over the next few years, my recollections are that this quickly disappeared. I don't know whether that was a result of the complacency that took over, but I recall, in looking back, that I began to indulge in habits that I don't recollect having before. One of those was smoking, which most of my brothers also did. In fact, I think they taught me so that I wouldn't tell on them. That vice got me into trouble often, at home and at school.

I used to have a job as a regular errand boy for a woman some doors away from us at Number 26 – Mrs Brown at Number 14, I think. Mrs Brown, locally known as 'Nanny', had only one leg and therefore used a crutch. I only got paid on a Friday or Saturday, 3d for the week. In between times Mrs Brown would give me the odd Craven 'A', she being one of the few women of the time who had started to smoke. This became almost a daily event and fuelled the bad habit. Mrs Brown was a great character of the period and locality, and like most people had an awful job making ends meet. I used to collect her groceries from one of several shops, depending on where she was creditworthy. When all the shops refused credit, she used to send me with a letter to the company offices for an advance sub – from Charlie's wages. Charlie was her husband. If I was successful, Charlie would only find out the following pay day when he went to collect his wages. I did not realise the part I was playing in these events at the time, but my mother could tell by asking me where I had been on any particular day for Mrs Brown.

I spent a lot of time when I was free from school in holidays, with the Henderson brothers from the Smallburn; Jock and Tam, I think, were their names. They had the contract for delivering parcels and other goods arriving in the village by railway. The transport was a horse-drawn lorry, which they would allow me to take charge of – under their guidance, of course. Muirkirk was well served by the railway in those days, having a locomotive depot, and situated at what was the end of the former Caledonian Railway branch from Lanark. There was a daily passenger service to Edinburgh along that line, and one to Ayr going west along a branch line of the former Glasgow and South-Western Railway.

I was not to know then what a significant part the railway was going to play in my working life.

As I said earlier, school life after age eleven did not seem to have the same attraction for me as I remember it having earlier. On reflection, I am sure this is a normal sequence as the lessons become more severe than they appeared before. In the knowledge that I would only be at school until I was fourteen years old and then likely look for a job in the pit like everyone else, I resigned myself to make the best of the three years until I could leave.

By the summer of 1937, when I was eleven, Jim, Hector and John were at work as far as I remember in the pits, Jim at Kennox in Lanarkshire and Hector and John at the Kames in Muirkirk. Boys leaving school were not long in getting work in the pits, because they were a source of cheap labour.

Having four workers out of a family of ten in two rooms pushed us well up the rehousing list. Our numbers, together with the fact that Dad was a right-hand man of John Colthart, a County Councillor, helped us to get rehoused in the 'Toon' in August 1939. We were to move to a semi-detached bungalow with three bedrooms, a living room, kitchen and bathroom.

It became the most exciting event in all our lives. Our accommodation was doubled, with a bathroom and kitchen added in. It was an indescribable time, more so for Mum, who by now had four of the family earning money, although Dad was a part-timer when it came to wage earning. He still had a high incidence of absence through injury rather than straightforward unemployment.

I was thirteen years old by the time we moved to our council house, and was much more conscious of what was going on around us, even world events that were prominent at that time. Even before 1939, I can remember the talk of the Spanish Civil War and the Italian invasion of Abyssinia and the German aggression in the countries of Central and Eastern Europe.

With the three older brothers at work, and the move to the

posh house, we could have claimed to have made it. But we'd beaten the poverty of the twenties only to be faced with what was to become the bloodiest and longest conflict of the century. It certainly was a period none of us is likely to forget. However, the short period when we were in the new house before the war began was then certainly the highlight of our lives.

It didn't last very long though, as Dad was still one of the first people to come to mind whenever there was an accident in the pit. Fathers with a son in the pit often got a place at the coal face, where big money could be earned, but invariably the danger increased. Dad got such a place with my brother Jim as his partner. Jim had moved from Kennox pit to the Kames.

Shortly after the war began in 1939, Dad had another of his accidents. This time Jim was working beside him when it happened. He suffered an extremely bad leg fracture in two places. It happened in the early evening, when they were on afternoon shift. Jim had never liked the pit, and that event helped him make the break with the pits. You could say it was a move from the frying pan to the fire, as he went next day and joined the Royal Air Force. Mum and the rest of us were not so sure, with the war already showing signs of being a long event, that Jim was improving his lot in getting out of the pit in exchange for joining the RAF. As it turned out, Jim did the wise thing and came through the war unscathed. He settled in Yorkshire, having got married to Edith, a farmer's daughter from Staxton, near Scarborough. They continue to live in Scarborough as I write in November 1992.

Jim and Edith have a daughter, Jean, and two sons, James and Stephen, and five or six grandchildren. As they are my eldest brother's family, I have a special affection for them all. I wish them good health and good fortune for the future, and hope they will get some pleasure from reading something of their family history, and the knowledge that their Dad suffered rough times in his childhood.

Dad was not destined to fare as fortunate as Jim did, as events were to prove. He was also sick from the series of accidents he had suffered over a number of years. That in itself over the years did nothing for the stability of the family, and I have no doubt it was Mum who suffered most through that period. Dad's solution to the accidents he had suffered from was similar to Jim's, in that when he recovered from his broken leg around the early part of 1940, he joined the merchant navy, having spent a period of his youth at sea.

It can be imagined how anxious a time Mum was now having, with her husband and eldest son in the services. After the severity of the twenty or so years prior to this time, things should have begun to ease. The move to a council house in 1939 appeared to suggest this was so. As I have said, the bright spell was short-lived. Jim's service was in the UK, and at least that eased Mum's anxieties compared to that of parents whose sons were abroad. Dad, however, was on the high seas at a time when lots of ships were being sunk, and he had at least one trip to America and another one when they were at Gibraltar. We used to get letters occasionally which conveyed news by way of a family code based on family birth dates – something like, 'I expect to be home a week after Andrew's birthday.' It was quite ingenious as it turned out, because letters from abroad were censored.

While Dad was away, I had reached my fourteenth birthday on 22 August 1940, and although I had a paper round which earned me six shillings a week (30p in today's money), I was anxious to have a proper job. I got a job at a farm a mile or so east of the village, Lightshaw Farm. The wage at the farm was thirty shillings (£1.50) a *month* – yes, a month – plus accommodation and food. Such were the good old days. I only worked at the farm for about three weeks before getting a job at Kennox pit near Glespin, a village seven miles east of Muirkirk; it was where Jim had started work. I remember being in the field gathering corn around seven thirty on a Saturday night during my three weeks at the farm. I think the low pay and long hours I experienced at the farm must have been a significant factor in my later involvement in Trade Union affairs.

My pay at the pit for six days a week – forty-eight hours as against about sixty-eight at the farm – was around £2 per week. That was nearly six times more than at the farm. I was really on my way. Nothing would stop me going to the very top. That was how I felt all those years ago.

I think a combination of the dangers of deep-sea voyages and Mum's anxiety made Dad decide, when he was home at the beginning of 1942, to take a job on a coaster. We were all a bit relieved at that because ship losses were then very high. I remember visiting Dad's coaster when he was in port at Ardrossan around that early part of 1942. Our relief was to be short-lived once more. His ship, the SS *Clermiston*, was in the Holy Loch, and Dad, being fond of his pint or three, went ashore with two of his mates. They apparently decided to row back to their ship by themselves, but the boat filled with water and all three of them were drowned. Dad and one of his mates were found almost immediately, but the third man was not found until about three months later. His accident-proneness had followed Dad to sea. The irony of that is almost unbelievable, unless of course you knew the Dodds family background. That happened on 30 June 1942, just two months before his forty-second birthday and Mum's fortieth birthday.

Poor Mum! Not yet forty years old, she was a widow with a family of eight to bring up. If life had been a struggle until now, it didn't look like it was going to be any easier in the future. Oh, for the good old days! This was really the beginning of the family breaking up, in the sense of not being together, and Dad having gone. Jim was away in the air force; Hector, who by now was twenty-one years old, was on the verge of getting married to Nan Park, and so he would shortly also be away; while Maisie had left school just before Dad's death and gone to work soon afterwards in the local Co-op.

I am sure we all missed Dad very much, perhaps the girls more so because they were younger. However, there did not appear such a closeness, particularly with a father of a big family in those days, as exists at present. This was not peculiar to our family at that time.

Matt had of course begun work before me, just after we had moved from the Rows to the council house in August 1939. Matt was the one male member of the family who never went to work in the pits. He actually started work on a farm between Muirkirk and Cronberry, called Stonebriggs. Like me later, he boarded at the farm; that way they could get more work hours out of you. I was well fed at my farm, but Matt was starved. Mum used to send me to Stonebriggs, mainly with food for Matt; and of course for me, still being at school, it was a novelty to be helping out with the work. For the farmer it was another source of cheap labour – in fact free labour. Oh, for the good old days! Shortly after Matt's farm job he got a job as a forestry worker, which he seemed to enjoy. He worked with an adult in woods that belonged to the pit company. Their job was to keep the pit supplied with the timbers needed for roofing in the coal-seams. Matt liked the outdoor life, although he was less fond of work than most, but at least he steered clear of the pits.

I was not long at the pit before I realised that it was not the job for me. I hated nearly every day I set out for work, having to travel the seven miles or so by the workmen's train. I left home at about 5.45 a.m. and got home at about 3.45 p.m. Because there was little work other than the pits in the district, the prospects of getting a job away from the pit was not bright. Another obstacle was Order 1305, the Essential Works Order, a wartime instrument governing the movement of people in industry.

One of my pals who also worked in the pit beside me was George Christie. George's dad was an engine driver at Muirkirk, and to get a job on the railway, you had to have one of your family or at least a close friend already working on the railway. George didn't want to work on the railway, and as I was his pal, his dad was prepared to speak for me for a vacancy as an engine cleaner at the engine shed.

Chapter Two

I got the offer of the job early in 1943, but then I was refused permission to leave the pit on account of the Essential Works Order Number 1305. It was supposed to apply only to those over seventeen years of age, but irrespective of the fact that I was only sixteen, the authorities were adamant that I could not be allowed to leave the pit. That was my first brush with red tape, and I badly needed my father to help me, but he had died nine months earlier. Our neighbour at that time, Hugh Love, took my case up with the local MP, and it was arranged that I would attend an Appeal Tribunal at Ayr against the decision not to let me leave the pit to work on the railway.

I succeeded in my appeal, which Mum attended with me, and the job on the railway had been kept open for me. I was really excited at the prospect of getting a job on the railway, with the probability of becoming a fireman and later an engine driver.

Before you could embark on this career you had to pass a fairly rigorous medical examination and an equally severe eyesight test in Glasgow. I passed both with flying colours, and started work in Muirkirk in May 1943 as an engine cleaner.

The wages of around £3 a week were similar to what I was getting at the pit, but here was a job I liked, and the future looked bright after the many hardships in my as yet young life. I was still too young to get working on the footplate – you had to be seventeen for that – so I was on night shift most of the time until my seventeenth birthday in August. The main reason for being on nights, although officially I was too young for that also, was to 'knock up' (waken) the early turn drivers and firemen an hour before they were due to report for work. In between times I had to clean engines and assist Jimmy Watson, who was the man on duty, to keep the engines in steam during the night. Jimmy and I became quite good friends, and he didn't have many. I think our friendship was partly due to the good chips I used to make for our supper.

Two vacancies for engine cleaners had been created at the small engine shed because two of the lads, a year or so older than me, left to join the air force flying crew. They were Andrew McSkimming and Jim McCartney. Andrew McSkimming was dead within a year, having been shot down, and while my recollections are not so clear, I think the same fate befell Jim McCartney. What a waste of young lives!

Two of my school classmates also became engine cleaners. They were Tom Hill and George Anderson. Tom Hill started just before me because he was not prevented from leaving the Kames pit as I was at Kennox. George Anderson started just after me, and a little later on George Christie changed his mind and joined us as well. We had a happy time together, and I soon reached the age where I was getting odd days on the footplate as a fireman. Tom Hill took up music and learned to play the saxophone. He formed a dance band in the village called the Modernaires, which George Christie and I became connected with. That is a story in itself, which I may manage to return to later in this narrative. George Christie did not continue his railway career; he is retired and lives in Kilmarnock still. George Anderson did continue his railway career, moving to Ayr, where he became a driver. He must now be retired as well. He lives in Kilmarnock.

I was not able to keep trace of Tom Hill because he left the railway to concentrate on his music and entered the professional music scene. The last I heard of him was when he went to South Africa, by which time he'd become a talented professional musician. A number of the former Modernaires did likewise, but as I said earlier that is a complete story in itself.

I suppose I ought to include that it was through the connection George Christie and I had with the band that he met Dorothy, his wife, and I met Margaret, who in turn became mine. George was manager of the band, in the administrative sense, booking halls in neighbouring villages in Ayrshire and organising the dances.

As George's main pal, I took on the role of his assistant. These were great times, even though the war was raging, and organising transport was a major task. Another member of the band in those days was Gerard Lang, who worked with me at the pit for some time. He and I spent a few days of our week's holidays from the pit in a small one-person tent in a farmer's field about seven miles on the Cumnock side of Ayr. We had a few cans of food (which was very scarce because of the war) and not more than £1.50 between us for our holiday. Oh, for the good old days!

I received a book from my sister Anna this year (1992) on the history of Muirkirk by Tom Findlay, which contains a section entitled 'The Success of Muirkirkians'. Gerard Lang features in that section thus:

> Ph.D., MBA (Master of Business Administration) Glasgow University; President and Chief Executive Officer of Misericordia Hospital, Edmonton, Alberta, Canada.

Very impressive for an ex-pit boy! Gerard's father, Mick, and mine were great friends, both very active in the Miners' Union. It goes without saying they liked a drink – together *or* apart.

I have a mention in the same section, three names earlier than Gerard on the same page, thus:

> Andrew Dodds, Assistant General Secretary, National Union of Railwaymen.

There are many others named in that section of the book who are much more impressive than either Gerard or I, but it feels good to be regarded as among those from Muirkirk who are worthy of getting a place in the history of the village. I spent the first twenty-three years of my life in Muirkirk, and though times were hard, my memories of the village are mainly happy ones.

I am sure that during some of these early experiences, such as that first holiday (when by the way we went on our bikes) with so little money, we would have wished at the time that things could have been better. Nevertheless they were experiences that taught us values we never forgot.

I was well into my adolescence by the middle of 1943, and nearly seventeen years of age. I felt happy with my job on the railway, and as it was regarded as a 'reserved occupation', I would not be called to serve in the forces unless I decided to volunteer. That was something I and my friends often talked about doing, and of course in the midst of the war you get a sort of feeling you ought to join up. There are also pressures on you from your family *not* to do so. This was no doubt due to the continual news in the village and in towns and villages generally about so many very young men having been killed. I didn't go into the forces, nor did any of my workmates.

When I reached seventeen years of age, I was able to take my turn at day and afternoon shifts. As I said earlier, this meant we got odd days acting as the fireman. On such occasions I felt very important, because in those days we ran passenger trains on the branch lines to Auchinleck, Ayr, Lanark, and on one turn we worked a through train from Ayr to Edinburgh as far as Carstairs. Carstairs was an important junction on the main line between Glasgow and England. Seeing the countryside during the different seasons was what made the job very interesting and satisfying for me. I began to look forward to going to work, a feeling I never had when I worked in the pit.

It was now about a year since Dad had been drowned, and the family had adjusted to our new situation. Jim and Hector had left home, so John was regarded as the breadwinner, with Matt, myself and Maisie also at work.

I am sure we all caused Mum some very anxious moments. We were all approaching adulthood, and she was having to cope with the problems which this development brought about. It did on a number of occasions cause fairly severe difficulties. I felt very sorry many times for Mum. I realise on reflection that the environment of the time made me more mature than my years. I felt it necessary to take on a protective role on behalf of Mum on occasions when family difficulties arose. John's lifestyle at one time caused problems in the family. We were lucky that these were only temporary difficulties.

John and Hector had been very active for some time in the local Communist Party. In fact while I worked at the pit they had me involved in the Young Communist Movement. The Communist Party was very popular generally at this time, but more so in Scotland's industrial and mining communities, and because of the attacks made on them by the Germans.

John had also followed in the footsteps of Dad, in that he was active in the Miners' Union, not only at local level but at district level also. In addition to his political and Union activities, he went to evening classes studying mining subjects. The village had produced some of the most eminent mining engineers in the country, and John did not intend to be a collier all his days. I will pick up this point later and will indicate how these studies brought about a major change in John's future.

I was beginning to show some interest in Union affairs at work, having joined the Railway Union shortly after starting employment on the railway in May 1943. I actually joined the National Union of Railwaymen in July 1943. I was not aware that there were different Unions in the railway industry, something that I will be eternally grateful for, as I might have joined the wrong Union. As far as the railway in Muirkirk was concerned, there was only *the* Union, that is the NUR. I was not to know then what a significant part the NUR was going to play in my life.

It seemed natural for the Dodds boys, including Hector (who was as much a Dodds as the rest of us), to be taking an interest in Trade Union matters. After all, our dad had been very active in the Ayrshire Miners' Federation. The strange thing was that Matt had absolutely no interest in Unions or politics. Matt was a keen fisherman and spent all his spare time fishing the different rivers in the district. John was also very keen on the fishing, and spent quite a lot of time at it too.

However, John had a hobby he preferred to fishing, which was cycling. There was an enthusiastic cycling club in the village, and they used to cycle great distances, even on a day trip basis. Lots of times they either camped out or used the youth hostels at weekends and on holidays.

Hobbies in those days had to be activities that did not involve a lot of expense. Fishing and cycling both fell into that category once you had initially equipped yourself. John bought himself a particularly good bike almost as soon as he started work around 1937–38. There was a local bike shop known as Willie Hunter's, and that was where John bought his new touring bike for about

£5, to be paid for in weekly instalments of two shillings a week (10p). He was very proud of that bike, as you can imagine. So were our Matt and I, and we were continually sneaking a ride on it. When our John caught us, there would be an almighty row. I referred earlier to the problems of bringing up a family which by now included a number of teenagers, and I was referring to incidents like this.

I soon decided that getting a ride on that smashing bike was not worth the hiding I was risking. Matt, then as now, was not so easily convinced and continued to make use of John's bike – or indeed anything else that he owned, like his clothes, or even mine. Poor Mum: she was the peacemaker in those difficult times, and used to try and persuade Matt not to cause trouble. Anyone who knows Matt even now would agree that he has never been inclined to do anything the easy way if it can be done with difficulty!

One of Dad's hobbies, as I mentioned, was poaching hares and rabbits, with snares or a dog. It was mainly out of necessity and a major contribution to feeding a big family. John, Matt and I took up this pastime also. John and I only went out occasionally, but for Matt it was almost an occupation. If the odd hen or chicken wandered by, it was likely to meet its end rather sooner than it expected.

Oh, for the good old days!

The family was maturing following the death of our father in June 1942, and me beginning work on the railway in May 1943. I was approaching seventeen years of age, Matt coming on nineteen, and John had turned twenty in March 1943. Maisie was fifteen and at work in the Co-op, but Anna and Betty were only twelve and ten respectively, and had some time to go before they were ready to leave school. John and Matt were of the age when girlfriends were prominent in their company. A favourite haunt of Matt's at that time was what we locally called 'The Dukes', between Muirkirk and Strathaven. It was in fact the Duke of Hamilton's estate, Dungavel, which around that time was an air force base, predominantly for the Women's Royal Air Force. Matt and a lot of his mates regularly attended dances there, and this was where he met a Strathaven girl, Betty Muir, who later became his wife. Betty was not in the forces, but was a factory worker in Strathaven, and one of the nicest girls you could have met. She was popular with the whole family, but sadly she had a stroke in her early forties, and although she made an initial recovery, she had a heart attack later and died about 1972.

John's girlfriends were usually from among the groups he associated with in his cycling club or through his political activity in the Communist Party. He soon had a regular girlfriend too called Annie Rankin. She hailed from Glespin. Annie, like Betty Muir, was an only child. I enjoyed the same pastimes as John and Matt, particularly the dances, but being a bit younger I did not have a steady girlfriend at this time.

It was not unusual late on a Saturday night, or more probably after midnight, to find that when I arrived home with my pal, George Christie, with the intention of him staying the night, my sisters had swapped rooms with us – we had two beds, they had one – because John's and/or Matt's girlfriends were staying the night. There was an accepted policy in our home on Saturday nights that those first in got the available beds.

My mother never knew until the Sunday morning how many she was going to cook for. They usually all had breakfast as they surfaced, but a headcount often had to be done before Mum started lunch. She never complained, no matter how many were there on a Sunday; in fact, the more there were the happier she seemed. She was wonderful, and it was mainly a very happy household during those years, despite all that had happened to the family, and the fact that the war was still raging in Europe and elsewhere.

Despite all the shortages during the height of the war, I don't recall those times causing us any great problem. We had become well used to our circumstances, which were the same for everybody. As a big family we probably fared better than most. Nobody ever got turned away from our house, and in fact lots of John's political and Trade Union colleagues from other places used to stay the night when they were at meetings in our village. They would do the same for John when the position was reversed. The Dodds' home had a reputation for hospitality. It started out when Dad had any of his cronies in the Union over from other places in Muirkirk. They certainly could not have got a bed in those days, but they could always get a meal. I am not sure how Mum did it, but she did. There was never a better provider than our mother was, and she maintained that reputation all her life.

Looking back on this period after Dad's death and my starting work on the railways until the end of the war in the summer of 1945, it now appears relatively uninteresting. I suppose it had something to do with the severe restrictions that there were on things we now take for granted. The only people then who travelled abroad, for instance, were people in the forces. I am sure many would rather have been at home, especially of course those who were taken prisoner. We were all very anxious for the war to end. I was thirteen years old when it started and was eighteen in August 1944, and would myself have been in the forces had it not been for the fact that I was working on the railway.

As it was for me, so it was for millions of others in that period. What an important but wasted period of so many young lives! I am not making a personal complaint, because compared to many who suffered extreme hardship in the actual fighting, some with terrible injuries and disablements, and many who were killed, I had had a cushy six years.

One incident I do recall vividly during the height of the German bombing of Clydebank is worth recording, as it is the nearest I ever got to the actual horror of war. As I remember, Clydebank was bombed for about three consecutive nights, the final one being on a Friday night. Mum had planned to go to Glasgow on the Saturday to buy a new dress for some occasion or other. She intending going on her own, but was a bit frightened to go on the Saturday daytime in case there was any more bombing during the day as well. Because she had been so looking forward to this trip, I said I would go with her for company. We left with the early bus, around 8 a.m. so that we would get away from Glasgow before it got dark. Mum got her dress and we had lunch in Lewis's for about 2s 6d each (12½p). We were making for a bus around 3 p.m. when the sirens began, indicating the start of an air raid. We were both frightened by now, especially when we saw the panic among the city dwellers scrambling on to any form of transport to get them out of the city.

As it happened, there was no further bombing that day, but the sirens were an indication of German planes perhaps photographing the havoc they had caused in the earlier raids. I shall never forget this experience, nor the pleasure Mum got from buying her new dress. Up until then her new dresses were few and far between.

I think that this was one of the occasions that led to a very close relationship that developed between Mum and me. John and Matt did not appear keen to take on the responsibilities of the man of the house after Dad's death. It was something I took on willingly when they got married, but I believe it began with that trip to Glasgow.

I got a big thrill out of accompanying Mum on that dangerous occasion. The girls would have been the natural partner for such an expedition, but Mum did not consider them old enough, especially with the risk from the air raids. It seemed she was happy with me for company, which made me feel quite important.

Anna was the next to leave school. She was fourteen in September 1944, and she soon went to work as well. She began in Stevenson's dairy in Cumnock, as I recall. Having two sisters working in food shops was quite rewarding in times of tight food rationing. When Anna went to work, the whole family – with the exception of Betty – were working, and the older ones were beginning to leave home to get married. First it was John and not much later it was Matt who tied the knot.

I was the man of the house then in my own right. I think I must have been looking forward to that happening. I think Maisie was also married by this time; she wed a very popular local soldier, Jackie Cowan. Jackie was a great fellow whom we all liked very much.

Some of the rooms in our bungalow had a problem of dampness that the Council couldn't seem to remedy, and as the family was shrinking through marriage, Mum wanted to move to a house with one room less but in the next street. She was keen on this move, and I took it on myself to go to the County Buildings House Department in Ayr and try and explain why my mother wanted to move. We hoped that giving up a bigger house would be in our favour. It seemed almost like a test to see if I was fit for the role of man of the house. The authorities agreed to our transfer, and the move took place.

George Christie's parents had moved to Kilmarnock about this time, and the Dodds household opened the doors to Geordie as a lodger. Here we were now with spare bed space. It seemed the natural thing to do as we were best friends and both working on the railway.

We were a very friendly crowd on the railway, and during the war period and for a time afterwards there were a number of women railway workers. Most of the signal box staff were women, as were most of the passenger train guards. The fitter's mate in the depot was Peggy McManus, a daughter of one of the drivers. It was common to find members of the same family working on the railway; in fact, it usually travelled through several generations. We often described it as a big family. In comparison to the numbers of workers in the pit, we were a very small organisation. That helped to create a very close community, and it really was as if we were part of a 'clan'.

Two of my close friends of the time at Muirkirk sheds were Willie Hamilton and Sandy Armstrong. They were drivers at the shed; Sandy was still only a fireman when I started in 1943, even though he had been on the railway since the early 1920s. Willie was already a driver, his father having been a driver before him and recently retired. He was a bachelor, and devoted his whole life to the railway. There was no formal training to become a driver in those days; each depot had its enthusiasts who organised training through what were called the MICs (Mutual Improvement Classes). Willie undertook that role at Muirkirk, aided by Sandy. They both took great pride in training us boys from the early days, even though it might appear to be some time before we needed to pass tests for driving. You were expected to have all this knowledge long before it was actually needed; it formed part of the rivalry that existed between the different depots in the area.

I was also becoming more involved in the Union, and really enjoying working life. It was unusual to have someone as young as me showing so much interest in the Union, but it came to me quite naturally. The older men of the time gave me every encouragement to becoming involved.

Shortly after the end of the war, the Territorial Army was reformed in the village, and for some reason or other I was attracted into it. It was not long before some of my pals from the railway also joined, including Geordie Christie, his cousin, and Jim Menzies who also worked on the railway. On reflection, it was not something that seemed to fit easily into my political and Trade Union views, and I remember often thinking at the time I had made a mistake. Like the army though, when you were in, that was it and you had to make the best of it. I did just that; I attended my training nights regularly, and some weekend camps. As time went by we all seemed to enjoy the Terries, and I remember attending at least two summer camps, one at Carnoustie and another at Hawick. After about a year of my two to three-year stint I got made a Lance Corporal. I think that was meant to try and encourage me to sign on for a further spell, but I never did. I must say I quite enjoyed my time in the Signals Platoon of the 4/5th Battalion of the Royal Scots Fusiliers. I expect it made me eligible to join the local British Legion club. I must remember that if I am stuck for something to do.

Springhill Terrace in Muirkirk around 1930. This was the family home after returning from Cambuslang following the birth of my sister Maisie in 1928.

Myself (far left) aged six with my four older brothers taken at school in about 1932. From left to right in ascending age are Matt (aged 8), John (nearly 10), Hector and Jim (nearly 11).

Top: Ayr Branch Colleagues making a retirement presentation to me at one of their many social functions during the Annual General Meeting in Ayr 1991. Margaret received a present as well. She was never left out.

Bottom: in the period between 1987 and retirement in 1991, I was the Union's representative on the British Rail Pensions Trustee Board, one of the largest pension funds in the country. I was also the first Trade Union chairman of the pension fund's management committee between 1990 and 1991, as shown in the Spring 1991 *Pensions Newsletter.*

Top: inaugural meeting of the Council of Executives NURMTW, 25 September 1990.
Bottom: myself and Neil Kinnock taken at the Labour Party Conference in Blackpool, October 1990.

Top: this is my identification label as an observer to the 11th Congress of the International Communist Trades Union held in East Berlin in 1986.
Bottom: invitation to the retirement of TGWU General Secretary Ron Todd.

Top: official certificate of thanks from the Labour Party.
Bottom: my documentation from the 1991 Labour Party Conference in Brighton.

Chapter Three

I remember the years after the end of the war in 1945 as being particularly active in various ways. We were all getting used to our new freedom of being adults in peacetime. There was still no extra food available, or indeed anything else, so that in this connection there was no difference between wartime and peacetime.

One other significant thing that did happen shortly after the end of the war was the General Election, which returned a Labour Government. I remember sitting in the bungalow late on the night the election results were declared. I was with Jim, who was on leave, and staying at home with Edith, his wife, and John, the political animal of the family. I was still only showing a little interest in these affairs, but I was getting a first-class explanation of what a Labour Government would mean from John.

I remember it as being very exciting, knowing that the pits, railways and other large organisations would come under state ownership. This was something our elders had dreamed about, and while it was not the first Labour Government in history it was the first one with a sufficient majority to carry out a full-blooded socialist policy. I would say these were my thoughts at the time, and no doubt those of millions of others as well. The dream did not last long, and though a terrific amount of good social legislation was put in place, the ingredient that was missing, which would have enabled a Labour Government to continue for many years more, was rank and file dedication to ensure the success of state ownership. There were too many of our own people undermining the system by taking more out than they were putting in, in addition to our enemies who were employed solely to bring the system into disrepute. I am not sure now, forty-seven years later, that we have learned the lesson.

Geordie and I spent a lot of time in connection with the

Modernaires band which I referred to earlier. George was more involved in it than I was, but we both went to neighbouring villages arranging dances for them to play at. As there were five or six of them, any organisation running a dance found them a bit expensive. Therefore, in order to get appearances, George and I would organise a dance somewhere, and take a chance of drawing enough money to cover the costs. That way the band got their appearance, which helped towards other engagements, but often there was very little surplus cash to pay them a fee. We had some real good times, but like the band it was never very financially rewarding. As has often been said, we did see life though. It was an activity that enlarged our circle of friends in the villages where the band played.

Our involvement with the band had to be fitted into shift working on the railway. The shifts, often late turns including Saturdays, made things a bit difficult, and meant a lot of organising with mates at work to be with the band. It was more important for Geordie to be there than me, so we were usually able to swap so that he was available. The band leader, Tom Hill, also worked at the shed and he had to be free from duty when the band had an engagement. John Wilson, another prominent member of the band, worked on the railway too.

Fortunately, John was a greaser in the C & W department and was on permanent day work. There was a distinct railway connection with the Modernaires between the band musicians and their administration. It seems they should have been called something like 'The Chattanoogans'. They were certainly one of the most popular groups of their day, and had they had modern techniques applied to them, they would have gone far. As it was, several of them became full-time professionals. Their pianist and arranger became pianist and arranger with the Lou Preager Orchestra, of Hammersmith Palais fame, in the 1950s. He was John Clark; he is now about sixty-two years old, and the last I heard of him, he was very deeply involved at the BBC. He lived near me in Harrow during the 1950s.

I have an interesting story to relate concerning John Wilson of the Modernaires which I will return to where it fits into the sequence of my story.

I mentioned earlier of how my brother John had been studying at evening classes concerning mining. He had obviously been intending one day to use this knowledge to improve his station in life, and not rely totally on improvements being brought about by his political activities.

During the latter part of the 1940s he got the chance of a supervisory or managerial position in ore mines in the Sinai part of Egypt. Although he had recently married, he decided to take up the position in Egypt. I had the advantage, as a railway worker, of having a certain amount of free rail journeys, and it was agreed that I would travel with John to see him off from Heathrow. He had to attend the offices of his company in London before leaving, to sign contracts and such. He had accommodation arranged for him and me for one or two nights at the Eccleston Bridge Hotel near Victoria.

We arranged to see *Annie Get your Gun*, one of the popular musicals running in the West End at that time. Dolores Gray and Howard Keel were the stars. The music was so popular (and still is) that it was like a dream being able to go there and see it in the flesh. I think about that event often, particularly when I listen to the music or see Howard Keel now after all these years.

I saw John away the following day and decided to go to another show before travelling back home overnight. My choice on this occasion was not so good. I let my Scots heritage influence me and went to see *Brigadoon*. It had some nice music but was nothing compared to *Annie Get your Gun*.

That trip to London with John in about 1948 or 1949 was my second to London. My first had been another momentous occasion in my life, the Scotland versus England match at Wembley on 12 April 1947. I got the chance of a ticket, and again, having free travel was considered to be almost equivalent to a millionaire. However in 1947, even though I was nearly twenty-one, a journey to London on one's own was frowned on. I had to find out who in the village was going to Wembley. It was as much a pilgrimage in those days as it is now. Scotland often held their own and sometimes won at Wembley as well. We found that one of the Boland family, Mick, and his pal, Willie Samson, were going to the match.

Mick was the brother of Bill Boland who later became a professional footballer with Glasgow Celtic. They were both a good few years older than me, but readily agreed to take me with them. They were meeting a local friend of theirs (then married and living in the London area) where they intended staying. The fact that I was from Muirkirk as well was regarded by them as being sufficient to get me on the guest list too. We met up with their friend, who I now know lived in Dunstable, and they assumed I was as welcome as they were. That was the reception from their friend; I am not sure it was reciprocated by his wife, who I think was English. Who could blame her, with a Scots husband and three mates from Scotland as guests during the International?

I think she gave a sigh of relief when the time came for us to set out for Scotland. It was a memorable weekend for me. Scotland drew 1–1, thanks to a goal scored by Jimmy Delaney of Celtic. Drawing at Wembley was considered a victory for Scotland, and like now, it was a biennial pilgrimage for lots of Scots. They saved for two years, just for that visit to Wembley. For a lot of the Scots supporters it was probably the only journey of any significance they had made since the previous visit to Wembley.

My social life was beginning to blend in with my increasing interest in the affairs of the Union. Will Parker, who was also a driver I used to work with fairly often, was the local branch secretary. He was keen to give it up, but was finding it difficult to get any of the other members of his age group to take over. With my background, to him I appeared a natural for the job.

Steadily, over a period of time, he got me more and more interested until I agreed to become the branch secretary. Sandy Armstrong and Willie Parker coached and looked after me until I was considered competent to be left on my own.

I was promoted to fireman from cleaner about May 1948. Although I had been acting as a fireman fairly regularly at that time, to be promoted to the grade of permanent fireman was a big step in my career. Muirkirk was a very small sub-depot from the parent depot of Hurlford near Kilmarnock, about twenty miles away.

There were only about eight drivers and eight firemen with about four or five cleaners at the shed. The four senior firemen were usually qualified drivers (passed firemen). Shortly after I became a permanent fireman, some of the senior passed firemen were promoted to drivers at other depots. That left only three passed firemen at the shed, and despite the fact I had only just been promoted to fireman, it was my turn to take the driver's test.

All the earlier training I had gone through with Willie Hamilton was planned for this very occasion. None of us ever thought it would come so soon, but it meant I quickly had to refresh all the teaching Willie had pumped into me earlier.

Nobody as young as me had ever been subjected to a train driver's test as far as we knew. A prerequisite to taking the test was to be medically examined and have your eyesight tested also. This was done at Rail Headquarters in Buchanan Street, Glasgow, and I was sent there in May 1949. In the course of the examination the doctor discovered I would not be twenty-three years old until August, and in those days you had to be twenty-three to be qualified to drive a steam train. I passed the medical and eyesight examination, but had to wait until my birthday to take the driver's exam. The consolation was that I had about three more months to ensure I passed my test. With all the coaching I was receiving it would have been a terrific let-down if I failed. I didn't let anybody down though, because after a two-day oral and practical examination, I passed with flying colours. Mr Watt, the inspector who took me through the exam, told Willie Hamilton and Sandy Armstrong that I had passed my test at a higher level than anyone he had tested before me. I have always been very proud of that tribute, although there is no record available to prove it. It also said a lot for the dedication of Willie Hamilton, who voluntarily undertook to train all my generation to pass the steam train driver's examination.

Willie is still living by himself in Muirkirk (November 1992) and is well over ninety years of age. I would like to take this opportunity of recording my gratitude for all that he did for me personally during those early years of my life in the railway industry.

Sandy Armstrong is another mentor who gave me great encouragement in all I attempted. So far as my career in the Union is concerned, nobody at Muirkirk did more to encourage me than Sandy. Sandy, like most of my elders from those days, has been dead for a number of years, but I want to pay tribute to his memory for all his encouragement to me to continue and progress my work in the Union.

Men like Willie and Sandy are hard to come by these days. The fact that I succeeded in the areas they encouraged me in was one way of thanking them for the time they spent coaching me.

I referred earlier to the connection with the Modernaires being the place where I first met Margaret Mitchell. The band played occasionally in Margaret's home town, Auchinleck, and sometimes in Cumnock, Catrine and Mauchline. Margaret worked in the optical works at Mauchline, and most of her friends worked there also. They came from the villages where the band played regularly, including Muirkirk. It was at one of the midweek dances in Cumnock that we first met, and our relationship developed from there over the next few years. What I didn't know until some time after I had met Margaret was that her father was the booking clerk at Auchinleck station. He had been there for many years, and his father had also been a railway worker. Sandy Armstrong knew Margaret's dad very well, and this was in the period when it usually did no harm for a father figure like Sandy to put in a good word for me.

Bob Mitchell was a highly respected member of the railway and local communities. He was a long time elder of the Barony Church in Auchinleck, where Margaret and I were later married. Bob also acted as a talent scout for Glasgow Rangers and for St Mirren. He was responsible for many young Ayrshire footballers getting their big chance with the famous Rangers, and one such that comes to mind was Eric Caldow who played for Muirkirk Juniors but came from Cumnock. Eric had a long and successful career, playing for Scotland many times.

Margaret's mother, Jemima, was equally well respected in the community, and it was fairly obvious to me at that time that I had begun a relationship with a girl from a highly respectable family. Auchinleck could not claim to be the most beautiful place in Ayrshire, but they had the best football team.

I was beginning to have a very full and active life. A qualified train driver at twenty-three years old, the youngest known at that time, I was secretary of the Union, and on the threshold of having a steady girlfriend. What did the song say? 'Who could ask for anything more?'

At home there was now only Anna, Betty and me besides Mum, as Maisie was also married. Betty had been at work since she left school at the end of 1946. She worked at the same factory as Margaret did in Mauchline, and she became part of the communications system we had to develop, as the phone was not common to many homes. I was still the 'man of the house', and I think helping Mum bring up the two younger girls was useful at the time.

Mum could see the time arriving when the rest of us would fly the nest as well as the older ones. As soon as Betty left school and started work, Mum began to look for a job as well. When Betty left school at the end of 1946, Mum had only turned forty-four years old. She was only entitled to ten shillings a week widow's pension because she was considered young enough to go out and earn her living. There were no extra points for having reared a big family – and that with the minimum of state assistance.

Mum had no difficulty in finding a job with her experience of domestic work – all of it practical. The Duke of Hamilton's estate, which had been a WRAF base during the war, later became a training school for the mining industry. Boys had the option of going to the pits instead of the forces after the war, and Mum got a job as a cook there. She later got the cook-in-charge job at Glaisnock Residential School in Cumnock, run by the County Council. All her ability – born of necessity – to provide food with the minimum of resources was now being recognised to her advantage. As I have said earlier, there was none better. When Mum worked at Dungavel, she was able to travel back and forth from home most of the time.

The seven years following Dad's accident had brought about a major transformation in our family. The four older boys were married, as was Maisie. John was in Egypt working, and Mum was a working grandmother, to Jim's first daughter, Jean, and to Hector's son, Jim. John and Annie had a child too, but sadly it did not survive. They adopted a newborn baby, Ian, in its place.

Now there was a real test of ability for me. Here I was, twenty-three years of age. I had left school nine years earlier at fourteen, the same time as I had actually spent at school. In those nine years since I had left school, I came to the conclusion that my formal schooling was to teach me how to learn. I had taken educational correspondence courses through the National Council of Labour Colleges in subjects like mathematics, English (for the purpose of writing reports, etc.), secretaryship and chairmanship. Nearly everyone of my generation intending to play an active part in TU or political affairs was encouraged to take some correspondence courses through the old NCLC, and they nearly all did so. Now was the chance to put to the test all the qualifications my NCLC certificates told me I had, in preparing a submission and presenting it to the Transport Users' Consultative Committee.

The procedure was the same then as it is now, i.e. you had to prove that withdrawal of the passenger service would create hardship in respect of named individuals. The case being considered was into the proposed closure of the Muirkirk/Auchinleck branch line for passenger services. This double line of about eleven miles had two morning trains to Auchinleck and an early evening one, with a morning train, an afternoon one and an early evening one back to Muirkirk. They were timed to connect with southbound trains travelling towards England, and northbound trains to Glasgow. There were only a very few people who used them regularly, which made it difficult to mount a case of hardship other than in respect of a few individuals.

Nevertheless, a lot of my training up to now had been on how to improvise and make the best use of the resources available. I certainly needed to do that now. I prepared all the material I had, such as the petitions and so on, and got ready to do battle with the TUCC.

Needless to say, although it was reported that I had put forward excellent arguments, I had not proved sufficient hardship to justify the withdrawal of the closure notice. The passenger service was withdrawn from the Muirkirk–Cumnock–Ayr branch at about the same time.

Although I had not succeeded in winning the case, I had apparently given a good display of my ability in presenting my argument. The whole exercise, lasting well over a year from the time notice of the closure was given, before the service was actually withdrawn, was my first experience of this kind. I learned a great deal during that period and became fairly well known in the district for the part that I had played, and met people from other walks of life. I learned also, if I didn't know before, that however big your problem is, someone near at hand will have a bigger problem than you. I came across several such people during our campaign.

It was a bit ironic that when the Auchinleck service was actually terminated following the last train on the Saturday evening to Muirkirk, I was the driver of it. Because there had been extra passenger trains on the Saturday, one or two of the passed firemen with a cleaner were used to make an extra crew, and this is what happened this particular Saturday evening. Margaret and her father and mother were passengers on that last train, having decided to use the occasion to visit Margaret's cousin, Peggy, who was married to Rab Parker, a Muirkirk man. I do not have an accurate record of all these events, but I think the Auchinleck service was withdrawn in 1950.

The fear we had of the possible effect of the withdrawal of the passenger services on the other work at our depot was justified. It was only because the Lanark branch passenger trains were maintained for quite a time after the withdrawal of the Auchinleck and the Ayr services that the coal train work continued at the depot for a bit longer.

The engine shed at Muirkirk had been insecure before the war, and it was only the outbreak of war that took away the threat of closure. A number of the staff did lose their job or had to move to other places to continue working on the railway following the events of 1950. From then on a number of us, myself included, did not have any confidence that we would be able to continue working on the railway far into the future, unless we were prepared to move to a depot with more security. The whole industry was showing signs of the aftermath of the war, and the nationalisation of the railways. Clearly, a Labour Government beginning its second term was not going to preserve the network they took under state ownership.

I was approaching my first adult crisis. My relationship with Margaret had developed to the point where we were planning to get married in about the middle of 1951. Security of employment has always been prized, but more particularly when you are planning to settle down to married life, with the likelihood of beginning a family shortly afterwards. True, there was plenty scope for continuing on the railway if you were prepared to move to other depots. Railway engine sheds were not as common as coal pits, with one at least in every village. There were only three engine sheds in Ayrshire at Ayr, Hurlford and Ardrossan. Moving away from Muirkirk around this time did not appeal to me.

I decided to tough it out at Muirkirk for the time being, and carry on with my plans to get married in the middle of 1951, as my role of 'man of the house' appeared to be nearly fulfilled.

Of my two sisters at home, Anna and Betty, Anna seemed as if she would soon get married to George Rowe. She had come back from working in Cumnock to work in the shop belonging to George's sister. George came back to the village, after spending the whole of the war years in the army, to join his brother Bill in the family garage business. Rowe's Garage was as much a part of the village as was the Kames pit. I think they were a bigger family than the Dodds, and the business had been there since horse-drawn vehicles were the norm.

Anna and George actually got married in June 1951, about a month before Margaret and me. We were married in the Mitchell family's church, the Barony, in Auchinleck on 25 July 1951.

Chapter Four

Our wedding was a very big event, Margaret being the only daughter of their family of two children. Drew, her brother, was my best man, and my sister Betty was Margaret's bridesmaid. Our reception was held in the Dumfries Arms Hotel in Cumnock, and of course I was proud to have Sandy Armstrong and Mary, his wife, as guests, together with my good friend, Willie Hamilton.

Margaret and I were considered lucky at the time, in that we had been allocated a rented railway-owned house about three weeks before we were actually married. The house was just over the fence from the engine shed. I never lived so near my work again until I became a full-time Union Organiser (I will explain that later). It was an upstairs flat of two rooms, similar to that which I had spent the first twelve years of my life. There I was, back living 'O'er the Water', after thirteen years in the 'Toon'. Having the house for three weeks or so before getting married was a boon. It was in good order, having been occupied by Hughie Bell and his wife; she was known locally as Lady Bell, because of her smart appearance and nice home. A railway guard in that time was considered a cut above a lot of villagers. My pals rallied round and we were able to strip the wallpaper and paint and paper it to Margaret's taste. We had some new furniture delivered, and this, together with all the presents we received, gave us a comfortable home to begin our married life in.

Margaret carried on working after our wedding, as we had planned, to enable us to save some money. Her factory, like others at the time, was suffering from lack of orders. About six months after we were married, a number of the girls were laid off, including Margaret. Although that upset our plans about saving in preparation for starting a family, it was for the best really, because it was too long a day with the amount of travelling. Margaret was leaving home shortly after 6 a.m. and travelling to the other side of Mauchline, a distance of nearly twenty miles, and therefore having to give that up was not such a great hardship. In any case, I was suffering from suspected stomach ulcers, even at twenty-six years of age, so Margaret being at home with me on shifts was of great benefit to me. We could also concentrate on beginning our family, which we both so much wanted, because compared to some of our friends we were late starters in this matter.

With the alteration to our circumstances brought about by Margaret's enforced unemployment, life for us was taking on a pattern that at least I was well used to, i.e. insecurity, as the threat to the railway persisted locally. However, we had our health and were ready to face the elements. We learned early in 1953 that Margaret was pregnant, the baby being due early in October.

Margaret had no major problems during her pregnancy through the summer of 1953, and at the end of September was taken to Irvine Central Hospital to await the arrival of our first baby. It was the nearest maternity hospital to our village, and was around forty miles away. It took me four hours of travel by bus to see Margaret for about forty-five minutes. Luckily we were not kept waiting too long before Margaret gave birth on 2 October 1953 to a bouncing baby girl whom we named Phyllis.

I am sure that from both Margaret's point of view and mine this was the most momentous occasion in our lives so far. Margaret was so desperate to have a baby, like many of her friends, and there never was any question that she would be one of the best mothers on earth. That she proved to be.

Early in 1954 I was made redundant; 'surplus to requirements', they called it in 1954. I was offered an equal position at either Ayr or Hurlford. I chose to go to Hurlford as advancement appeared a better prospect there than it did at Ayr. In the first month or so it was difficult travelling for a pattern of twelve different shifts, many of them in the middle of the night. I had no personal transport so I was always relying on swaps. That was not too difficult because the most unsociable shifts were also the ones where you earned extra pay, and many of my new colleagues, young married men with families, were keen on the extra money.

Sometimes I stayed away from home. At odd times I stayed

with the parents of my friend, George Christie, in Bonnyton Square, Kilmarnock.

It was not too long before I was allocated a two-apartment ground-floor BR house, also in Bonnyton Square, Kilmarnock. It was like heaven; we had our own inside toilet, and soon after were able to have a hot water geyser installed over the sink. Phyllis was making good progress and experienced her first house move before she was one year old. We settled down quickly, made friends and renewed other friendships. Margaret soon made friends through George Christie's wife, Dorothy, who knew a wide circle of people, and most of them had babies around the same age as Phyllis.

I was soon into Trade Union activity in the local Hurlford branch of the NUR, and became the branch chairman soon after I joined. This rapid promotion was due then to the chairman, Bob Banks, being a senior Kilmarnock Town Councillor and soon to become the town Provost. My activities within the NUR at branch and district level were known at Hurlford, and to them I seemed a gift. There were just as few volunteers for Union positions then as there are now, so any who did volunteer – like me – were quickly snapped up.

Through Bob Bank's interest in me as a young active Trade Unionist, he introduced me to local politics, and it was not long before I was standing as a candidate for the Labour Party in the Town Council Elections. I stood in a couple of elections unsuccessfully soon after arriving in Kilmarnock.

Being a member of the larger Union branch at Hurlford than the one at Muirkirk gave me opportunities for greater activity, and it was not long before I was a delegate to the Glasgow and West of Scotland District Council of the NUR, and to that body's Loco Grade Committee. In fact, around 1954 I was elected to the District Council Executive Committee, apparently the first member from outside Glasgow itself to become a member of the Executive Committee.

Hurlford was a fairly large loco depot, having about four hundred footplate staff, about 305 of whom were members of the Associated Society of Locomotive Engineers & Firemen. The big majority of the other twenty per cent who belonged to the NUR were former ASLEF members who had fallen out for a variety of reasons. There were a minority of NUR members like me, who were NUR members from the start of their railway service. The local leaders of the Loco Union did not take kindly to me therefore when I started to recruit some of the new entrants, i.e. engine cleaners. Prior to my arrival at the depot they used to leave the new entrants for a few weeks before signing them up for their Union because there was nobody from the NUR in the depot opposing them. Naturally they did not like my actions, especially when I recruited a few of the new recruits, and even poached a few of their existing members. The depot representatives were three from ASLEF, representing all footplate staff including cleaners, and an NUR representative for all non-footplate staff. I insisted that this body arrange open meetings for all staff to hear reports of their deliberations with management.

I was also able to put forward non-controversial suggestions which were taken up for future discussions with management. I was beginning to make my mark within the depot and livened up even the existing NUR members. It was a great pity, therefore, that within a year of me arriving at Hurlford a serious national industrial dispute resulted in ASLEF calling a strike; while the NUR, who had settled their wage dispute through the famous Cameron Inquiry, instructed their loco members to work normally, but obviously to do only their own work. The majority of the NUR loco members at Hurlford joined ASLEF and took part in the strike, a lot of that due to the high level of intimidation that took place in a very close-knit community.

As Chairman of the local NUR branch, I, together with about some ten or so others, followed the NUR line to the letter. We were subjected to horrendous behaviour, some of it physical, for the whole of the seventeen days that the strike lasted in June 1955. My baby daughter, Phyllis, who was just under two, was treated equally badly by neighbours who wouldn't talk to her. Fortunately she was too young to understand what it was all about, but Margaret suffered similarly from neighbours who two weeks earlier had been our friends. Margaret supported my stand to the hilt, and because we were in Kilmarnock and not in the close-knit community at Hurlford, who were mainly loco workers, we soldiered on. On reflection, I believe the NUR policy of instructing their members to work normally was wrong; to me they would have come out of the dispute stronger if they had publicly indicated their opposition to the dispute, as being *sectionalist*, while at the same time instructing their members to stay away from work in the interest of *workers' solidarity*.

The dispute ended after seventeen days with minor concessions to drivers, with the firemen and cleaners getting nothing.

The NUR numbers at Hurlford were down to a mere dozen or so, and nationally the Union lost a large number of members. The ensuing years were spent trying to rebuild our loco membership base.

As could be expected, local feeling within the depot after the resumption of work was very bad among a large number of ASLEF members, who in my opinion had been let down by their Union. The NUR and its loco members were to become the whipping boys, and most of us were sent to Coventry, together with our families. To anyone not used to the term 'sent to Coventry', it meant not being spoken to, at least; but to many of the more militant ASLEF members it went well beyond that and included physical violence.

As the local NUR chairman, I was subjected to a lot of aggravation, such as having sugar added to the petrol tank of the little motorbike I had acquired to travel back and forth from home to the depot, about four miles away. That ruined the bike and made me rely on getting lifts on light engines between Kilmarnock and the depot at Hurlford, and from the depot to Kilmarnock. Most of the ASLEF drivers reluctantly allowed me to travel, because it was a local custom and to stop me would have meant many of the colleagues would not have been able to travel either, because it was all *unofficial*; but management turned a blind eye to it.

One of the more militant ASLEF drivers decided to refuse to allow me on an engine travelling from the depot to Kilmarnock, although he had about six ASLEF and NUR members on board. I decided to insist on joining them, whereat he aimed a blow at me with the coal hammer (a large, long-handled pick). He only grazed the side of my face, luckily for me, because a direct hit would almost certainly have killed me.

I naturally left the loco and went back to the depot to report the incident. The police interviewed me and took the evidence I have just related, including the names of the witnesses on the engine at the time. The ASLEF members denied having seen anything of the incident, and even two active NUR members who were on the loco were very reluctant to offer evidence to support my complaint. In fact, one of them refused point blank to give any information, and when the ASLEF driver was charged with assault at the Magistrate's Court he was brought there as a hostile witness. The NUR gave me every assistance from Headquarters, and indeed arranged for me to be interviewed by their Scottish solicitor from Glasgow, the redoubtable Bill McPhail, whom I already knew slightly. I can still remember that interview yet in Bill's office in Glasgow. He gave me such a grilling about the details that I felt that it was me who was on trial. Bill treated me like the brother he was to the NUR, and was present with me at the trial, and on a number of occasions before it, to reassure me. Because of the reluctance of witnesses to give evidence to support what they had clearly seen, the outcome was a verdict of 'Not Proven'.

The experience did not stop the man concerned from continuing to try and intimidate me, until one day when his regular fireman did not turn up for duty early in the morning. I was a spare fireman and was sent with this driver to work a passenger train to Glasgow. This was the opportunity I had waited months for – getting on a footplate with this particular driver. It was just him and me for the next six hours or so. Like all bullies, he was one of the biggest cowards under the sun. I did not adopt any physical retribution, because that would have gone against me very badly. I was much more subtle and just set out to make his life a misery that day through, not putting water in the boiler or coal in the fire until he instructed me.

The aggravation of the past year or so had not helped my stomach ulcer problem and my doctor said this was not being helped by shift work and irregular meals. A vacancy on the clerical staff was advertised at our depot and I decided to apply for it. I had to sit an exam, which I passed, and was offered the position, which I took. It provided me with a regular nine-to-five job, but it had a restraining effect on my Union activity.

Around this time I was allocated a council flat in Onthank, a nice part of Kilmarnock, and I had no hesitation in accepting it. It had two bedrooms, a bathroom and a kitchen, and you can imagine how nice that was compared to where we began in 1951, with two rooms and an outside shared toilet. A change of job and a new flat seemed too much to be true.

Phyllis was developing by this time, 1957, and was very bright for her age. Soon she would be starting school, and of course Margaret was planning to add to the family because she was quite intent on having several children.

I continued my Trade Union activity and also became more involved in local politics. As I stated before, I stood unsuccessfully in a number of elections. Then suddenly an NUR councillor died; the practice in Scotland was that, instead of having a by-election, the party who held the seat were allowed to co-opt a representative to fill the remaining period of office of the person elected. The local Labour Party chose me for that vacancy, and so late in 1959 I became a Kilmarnock Town Councillor.

I was not comfortable in the clerical position I had gained and was watching for an opportunity to make a move. The NUR Headquarters around that time were advertising positions on the administration staff at Unity House in London. I had often seen those positions advertised in the past and had set my sights on one. However, they wanted people not more than thirty years old, so it looked as if that door was closed.

The addition to our family that we were planning took form, Margaret becoming pregnant around April 1959. Phyllis had started school almost across from our flat soon after we had arrived in Onthank; that would be the end of the summer, 1958. It seemed to be the signal for Margaret wanting an addition, because she had devoted all her time to Phyllis, with good effect on both sides. Phyllis must have been one of the brightest children of her age, from the time she started walking, which in itself was before she was a year old. She chatted to everybody, very intelligently, from an early age. No doubt Margaret was missing her company when she began school in September 1958. I think that is what Margaret felt when she became pregnant in the spring of the following year, 1959.

The addition to the family we had planned arrived on 22 January 1960 – another lovely baby girl, whom we named Alison. I remember going over to the school around their break time to tell Phyllis she had a sister. Alison was born around eight o'clock that morning. Phyllis was very excited as well as me and spent the rest of the day telling everyone about her new sister.

The prospect of getting a position at Union Headquarters in London arose again towards the end of 1959. They had decided to increase the age of recruits to thirty-nine, which made me eligible. I applied for one of the vacancies and was invited to London to sit an examination on the same date that I was due to attend my first meeting as a Town Councillor. I asked the NUR to alter the date, but they explained that that was not possible as there were more than one hundred people sitting the examination for around twelve vacancies. I felt in the circumstances that I had to withdraw my application and informed them of that decision. I was also influenced in this decision by the arrival of Alison. Something that I had longed for coincided with another thing I wanted, a second child.

I resigned myself to getting on with life in Kilmarnock with my new white-collar job, two lovely daughters and a wife second to none. I was not unhappy with my lot. Then, out of the blue, came a letter from NUR Headquarters telling me one of the original applicants had fallen sick on the examination date, and they had arranged a new date for him to take the exam. In the circumstances, they invited me to join him on this new date. As it did not clash with anything, I accepted the invitation. I passed the exam as first equal out of the one hundred or so applicants and I was offered a position.

Margaret and I spent the following week discussing well into each night whether I should accept the position or not. It was and still stands as the biggest problem we had ever faced. A week after the offer was made, and near the deadline for accepting, I still could not make up my mind. I was thinking how unfair it would be to go off to London leaving Margaret with two young children. Margaret told me to make a decision and whatever it was she would support it. She had always been a tower of strength to me in all my activities. On the final day for the decision I resolved to accept the position in London and informed my boss at Hurlford on that Saturday morning. He told me to finish there and then, take the following week as holiday and prepare for my new job in London.

The week of my holiday was spent tying up all the loose ends of my activities in Kilmarnock, in the Trade Union and as Town Councillor. I had to resign from the Council a little over a month after I had been appointed. I am sure I hold the record in Kilmarnock, if not in Scotland, for having served the shortest time of anyone ever as a Town Councillor.

Everybody concerned saw my move as a big step and gave me full encouragement in my decision. Unknown to me, this was the beginning of a high-flying career in the Trade Union Movement.

I am sure that, when I left Kilmarnock for this new job in London, around 2 March 1960, I did not realise the magnitude of what I had decided to do. Margaret was left in Kilmarnock with a two-month-old baby and a daughter of six and a half who was very close to me. Phyllis used to spend hours sitting with me, combing my hair (which I had in abundance then) preparing for her and me to go to London. Phyllis had been in London on the way back from a south coast holiday, and whether that was the background to this game we played or not I will never know, but here I was going off on my own.

I suppose it helped when I arrived to find there were several others like me from the provinces who had accepted positions, among them my good friends, Bill Grealey from Stockport and Len Bound from Blyth. Both of them had left families behind them, but none were as young as mine. Having that in common we became close friends, and our friendship lasted a lifetime. Sadly, both Bill and Len have gone to the other side.

We shared lodgings for some time, getting paid a travel allowance once a month to visit home. Bill was fortunate in that he got an exchange of council house to Brixton within a month or so. Shortly afterwards, Len got a house in Ruislip, Middlesex, which he had to buy. The Union started a scheme whereby they granted a mortgage at low interest compared to building societies. This we took advantage of. All three of us were attending evening school to qualify in typing and shorthand, which we were told would be necessary to get promotion.

I eventually got a house also in South Harrow towards the end of September 1960. Margaret had come to London with Phyllis and Alison in July 1960 to help me look for a place. Our dear Aunt Margaret, who lived in Hounslow, had invited Margaret and the children to come and stay in order to have the opportunity of looking at houses. What a dear she was then, and proved to be for the next thirty years. Not long after Margaret's two-week stay without finding a house, one became available in South Harrow. Margaret could not see it, but she agreed I should take it if in my opinion it appeared suitable.

Although the house I had found was not very outstanding, it was the best I had seen in about three or four months of looking. It was in a good commuter area, about forty minutes to the office by tube, and was as much as I felt I could afford: £3,200. I kept in mind that my annual salary was £620 and that the house was going to bring an end to our separation as a family after six long months.

We actually moved in around the middle of October, on the most dismal day you could imagine, with rain falling heavily. We were up to our knees in leaves from the trees which grew next to the house. The interior was in severe need of redecoration. Coming there from a nice bright flat in Kilmarnock, and being so far from home, was not going to make settling in easy for Margaret. It was very difficult for a while, but Margaret made the best of it. As her mother was able to travel free by rail, she visited quite a lot, thus easing the position for Margaret in the early days.

We soon found that buying a house created its own financial problems, and I had to look for a part-time evening job. That was to be in a pub, and I was lucky in getting one in Harrow, only fifteen minutes from home. The small amount of extra money from two or three nights at the pub was a godsend, as by then I had an old banger I was trying to run.

I was also having to attend night school two nights a week throughout the winter to get the qualifications necessary for promotion. That and the part-time job those first two years did not leave me with much more time with the family than I had before we all came together to Harrow. We were determined to make a go of it, however, and everybody played their part. Phyllis settled in at school after a short time when her classmates took the mickey out of her for her Scots accent. Even in those days, Phyllis was a resourceful girl and soon got on top of it. Alison was thriving, and Margaret had a busy life rearing them. But it was a tough two years until the end of 1962.

Early in 1962 we had numerous visitors from Scotland to stay with us. I suppose those friends and family who came found it a great novelty being able to visit acquaintances so close to central London. While it created some extra work for Margaret, we both enjoyed the contact.

Among our early visitors were Willie and Jenny Christie, the parents of my best friend, George Christie. Willie particularly had been like a father to me for most of my time on the railway, and he was already at Hurlford when I arrived there in 1954. He did a lot for me then, and to have him as our guest was a pleasure and went some way towards repaying him and Mrs Christie for their kindness to us.

George, my friend, and his wife, Dorothy, also came and stayed, which again gave us a lot of pleasure. George had another friend living two streets away, also from Muirkirk. He was John Clark, a professional pianist with the famous Lou Preager dance band of those days. John had been pianist with the Modernaires from Muirkirk. George had acted as their engagements manager, with me as an unpaid assistant, as I mentioned earlier.

My adopted brother, Hector, also came in the summer of 1962 with Nan, his wife. He loved popular music and musical shows and saw a few of them in London during his stay. Hector and I had always had a close relationship, and it was a great joy to have him and Nan with us. He was a lovely man, and Margaret had a great affection for him as well.

Margaret was kept busy that first summer, because it seemed as soon as one lot of visitors went another lot arrived. We only had one spare bedroom, so it was quite a job getting things in order for visitors, bearing in mind that we were trying to decorate the place as well. It was difficult at the time with the two young girls, but I think it helped Margaret overcome the violent change we experienced in our move from Scotland. I was at work all day among new friends, so for me it was easy.

We were settling down to our new life in London, and getting the odd visit back home to see our respective families. My mother was still working as a cook, as she had done in various educational places in Ayrshire for a number of years. By now she had been the school kitchen cook in Muirkirk for quite some time. My God, if ever a woman had a hard life it was my mother! She was widowed just a couple of months short of her fortieth birthday. Once the girls had started work, the then equivalent of the Social Security told her she was young enough to get a job, and provided only the basic widow's pension, which was a pittance. She was skilled at most things – dressmaking, knitting, decorating, and acting as midwife when other neighbours had their children at home.

Getting a job as a cook was easy for her, because she had had to do that for a big family all her life, and with very little money available. We never went hungry though. Being a cook where food was provided in plenty was easy compared with earlier life. She was first in the former Duke of Hamilton's estate, which during and after the war was a training establishment for 'Bevin Boys' or pit trainees. These were named after Ernest Bevin, the former Minister of Labour. From there she went to Glaisnock House, another residential college connected with the farming industry in Cumnock, and then to Muirkirk.

My mother was a very proud lady and loved nothing better than seeing her family getting on in life. She was so proud when I got the job in London; being the youngest of the boys, I suppose there was something a bit special about me as far as she was concerned. It probably developed because I was the one who helped domestically when the girls were too young to assist her in that way. I continued taking some of the responsibility after the older brothers got married and left home.

Before I left for London in 1960, John had gone to work in Egypt and West Africa and Matt was a partner in a road haulage firm. Mother was very proud of all of us, the girls included. It was a delight when she decided to come and have a holiday with me in the summer of 1962. Before her visit, however, Hector was planning to come that summer again too, and one day in March 1962 I had a letter from Hector 'booking' his room for July. Later that same day I got a message in our office telling me that Hector had been killed by an explosion in the Kames pit. He would only have been past his fortieth birthday that January, and he left two children. What a tragedy to befall our family, especially after what had happened to our father in the pit and then at sea.

My mother did get her visit to us that summer, and she brought one of her many grandchildren, Lynn Cowan (Maisie's daughter), with her for company. Mother had never been in London before, therefore I tried to show her as many of the tourist attractions as I could: the House of Commons, Buckingham Palace, Number 10, Downing Street, and the National Gallery, where the Mona Lisa was on exhibition. We also took in a little shopping in Oxford Street and Regent Street. That was all in one day! She was thrilled but exhausted when we got home.

I think all the grandchildren had been born by that time, and if so there were twenty-three of them altogether.

The events of Mum's life that I have described must have started to take their toll, because unbeknown to me she had been complaining for some time about what she thought was severe indigestion (stomach ulcers, more likely, which she already had). It was another shock therefore when I got a message, again in the office, on the morning of 27 November 1963 to tell me that Mum had had a massive heart attack and died.

So ended the life of a wonderful mother. No one of her generation could have worked harder in rearing a big family single-handedly. What a great pity she was not spared to enjoy some of the fruits of the prosperity she played a big part in creating for her family.

Hector's tragic death, followed so soon by my mother's death, made me very angry. It seemed as if a curse had descended on the Dodds family.

Chapter Five

However, by now I had gained the shorthand and typing qualifications I needed, and I was promoted to be a section clerk in charge of the branch accounts section in the Finance Department, where I had begun my Head Office career two and a half years earlier. As it brought a good increase in salary, I was able to give up my part-time job and spend more time with the family. We were also able to buy a better car, a Morris Minor, which proved we were on our way.

At this time I was heavily involved in staff affairs in the office, having been elected staff chairman. I was continuing my activity at branch level in the Union, and became secretary of the Harrow and Wealdstone branch, and was also active in the West Harrow Constituency Labour Party. It was as if nothing had changed from my time in Kilmarnock as far as those matters were concerned.

Through my position in charge of branch affairs in the office, I got to know a great many of the then 1,700 branch secretaries. It was mainly through talking to them on the phone, but a lot of the London area secretaries would visit the office with their problems, so I got to know a lot of them personally. I also developed a good relationship with most of the divisional organisers. I was thoroughly enjoying my job and at that time expected to progress to higher stages in the administration staff.

In early 1966, vacancies arose for two divisional organisers. Roy Maunder, a friendly Executive Committee member representing bus members, asked if I would coach him on how to compile a branch balance sheet and in other matters of branch affairs. These formed a large part of the examination that candidates for organiser had to pass as one part of the selection process.

They had to have a seventy-five per cent pass in two separate parts of the examination before they could be included in the ballot. The other part of the exam was demonstrating knowledge of Union–employer agreements through answering a series of written questions.

I readily agreed to assist Roy, but at the same time saw an opportunity to seek election as an organiser too, which I was still entitled to do even though I was a staff member. I already was an acknowledged expert in branch financial affairs and had a reasonable knowledge of Union–employer agreements, particularly railway agreements. I spoke to some active colleagues about my thoughts in this direction and received a lot of encouragement by way of promised nominations, at least to enable me to take the examination.

I got a respectable number of nominations, took the test and came second in the ensuing ballot, thereby securing the vacancy for the second of the two positions. I am pleased to say Roy Maunder also passed and, although not successful in that election, was elected a short time later.

I was a real dark horse in securing election, so much so, that the then General Secretary, Sidney Greene, later Lord Greene, sent for me the day the result was announced to tell me how pleased he was, even though he was greatly surprised at my beating so many well-known candidates, who were customarily former Executive Committee members.

I was only the second member of staff ever to have been elected an Officer, the previous one having become an Assistant General Secretary. I had won by six votes after several recounts. Jack Lanwarne, whom I beat by those six votes, was heard to say, 'Andy who?' when told my name. So he might have been the originator of that famous phrase.

Shortly before the election, a semi-detached house became available next door to a Scottish family in Pinner, Alex and Jean Turnbull, whom Margaret had became friendly with after meeting them at the United Reformed Church. Jean was keen to have Margaret as a neighbour, and Margaret was keen on the prospect of a move. It was only a couple of miles away, but to a nicer area. Although at that time I had received a boost to my salary through promotion in the office, I was not sure we could raise the extra cash for a more expensive house. Nevertheless I decided to try and get my bank to loan me the extra money. The bank agreed and the move came off.

There I was, four and a half years after arriving in London as a clerical officer on the Union's administration staff, having been elected against long odds to become one of twenty elected Officers of a major Trade Union representing around 200,000 members, and I'd just reached my fortieth birthday. My salary doubled, enabling me to absorb the increased cost of the house move, and indeed to install the central heating. The anguish we went through in deciding whether or not to come to London at all in 1960 suddenly seemed unjustified. Our decision was proved to be right. Although I don't suppose I realised it at the time, I was well in line to become the leader of the Union in due course. This was a view expressed to me by colleagues already in position as organisers, based on the age and seniority profile among all those in position before me. The positions of General Secretary and Assistant General Secretary, although subject to further examination and election, had nearly always followed a 'Buggins's turn' principle. That was the future though; it was the present that was important.

My one regret was that my mother had not been alive when I was elected. She would have been so proud.

I took up the appointment in October 1966, initially as road transport organiser, which in practice meant you were a relief Divisional Officer as much as dealing with road transport matters. Further spells away from home appeared to loom, and in fact I did spend two periods of a few months away from home during the week. The first was a two-month spell covering the Birmingham district, when I lodged in Warwick.

I was then sent to Exeter to cover Devon, Cornwall, Somerset and part of Hampshire, where there was a big bus membership. Having to be away from home during the week was a big sacrifice again, with the girls growing up fast, but it was a great opportunity to get the confidence needed to make a successful organiser. My good friend and fellow Scot, Bill Murphy, the Resident Officer in Exeter, taught me a lot about the responsibility of the position when I was sent to work with him for about four weeks immediately after my appointment.

It was sad that so soon after that initial training, I had to cover Bill's district when he had a stroke while on holiday in Romania. He died a few months after that event in 1967, and for a time it looked like I might become the Resident Officer in that district.

However, another fellow Scot, Alex Shearer, organiser for London South, Kent, Surrey and Sussex, died suddenly. I opted for that district and was appointed to it towards the end of 1967. My good friend Roy Maunder, who by this time had been elected an organiser, took over the Exeter district, as he was then resident in Torquay.

My appointment to the London South area meant another move of home to somewhere south of the Thames, but within twenty miles or so of London. After considering all the options we chose a new three-bedroom detached house being built on a small estate in Selsdon, South Croydon, which was planned to be completed by the middle of 1968. The house was a long way from being completed when Phyllis was due to start her new school after the summer holidays in 1968 (Archbishop Tennison's) where she was accepted. I had to put Phyllis into a small hotel near her school between Monday and Friday for her to get the benefit of the beginning of a term. Getting Phyllis there on Monday at 9 a.m. and arranging to pick her up around 4 p.m. was a mammoth task, but we did it fairly successfully until December.

We eventually moved into our new home in Selsdon in December 1968, some six months later than expected, and a year after I had taken over as Officer for the district. I certainly found a great benefit in that I was actually living near where a lot of my work was taking place.

We were back together as a family again, and with the social activity that went on among the branches in my district, Margaret and the girls quickly became part of the big NUR family, because they were always included in any invitation to social functions which came to me. Margaret, as always, proved to be very popular.

It is difficult to single out individuals for praise because there were so many that deserved it, but one who was totally devoted to the Union, and still is, even though he has long since retired, was Les Roberts, together with his wife, Bett, and all their family.

There was not a family occasion, wedding, christening or anything else in the Roberts family that Margaret and I were not invited to. In fact we still get invited to their family occasions. Well done, Les and Bett.

I had been well received as the Officer, especially as I had succeeded another Scot. I quickly got to know the branch secretaries, around seventy of them, and had good relations with the three district council secretaries: Tim Young, in the South-East, Paddy McGinty in the Southern and Charlie George in the South-West. They were all very helpful and thoroughly loyal to the Union and its Officers. The same cannot be said at the present time.

To make a success of the position on behalf of the members, relationships had to be developed with personnel managers too, and in the main I was able to accomplish that in a way that gained respect not just for me but for the Union. After all, I was only the representative of the Union, and the Union was its members.

During my time in the district, from 1967 to 1975, Phyllis reached school leaving age in 1970. She gained a few O levels but did not want to continue at school. She was not sure what kind of job she wanted other than to say she did not want a regular nine-to-five office-type job. I suggested she might consider something on the railway, as I had done and as her paternal grandfather had done. In fact, Margaret's dad had spent his whole working life, forty-eight years, as a railway booking clerk, a highly respected profession in those days. Phyllis decided that she would try for a job in the industry, and fancied a position as a hostess on the Gatwick trains from Victoria. Phyllis was still too young for those positions, but was offered a junior clerk's position in the Information Office at Victoria until she was old enough to get a hostess position. She took the offer and thus became the third generation of the family to begin a career on the railway.

Phyllis's career proved to be brilliant and took her eventually high up the management structure. She quickly moved out of Victoria after a few years, and went to work as a hostess with Hovercraft, based at Charing Cross. In a short time she gained a position as a sales representative for them, her first move into managerial grades. During that time she met John Cooper, who was a management trainee, and in 1979 they got married.

John was given his first appointment after training as Station Manager at Chislehurst and Elmstead Woods. They took up residence in Orpington, which was suitable for them both in their respective jobs. John was offered a move to Battle in East Sussex. This he was not keen on; it would have created difficulties for Phyllis getting to work as she did shifts. He felt that by refusing the offer his future was suffering, and he decided to leave the railway.

John's decision to leave was probably influenced by me, as I knew they were looking for administration officers in our Headquarters, and he was admirably suited for such a position. Without Head Office knowing the relationship between John and me, he applied for a position and was successful. Phyllis had joined the NUR when she took her first railway job, even though that was not fashionable among white-collar staff, most preferring the white-collar Union, the TSSA, which her grandfather had belonged to. John, now working for the NUR, also became a member of the NUR, having previously been in the TSSA when on the railway. I had gained two new NUR members in my family.

Phyllis made another move, this time into the Press and Publicity Department at Waterloo. In that position she used to broadcast train information on local LBC radio and became quite well known through her voice. She broke into an area which had been largely a male-dominated one, but quickly showed she had ability which could not be kept back.

John became disillusioned at NUR Headquarters and decided to seek a career in business management, which is what he had been trained for. He got a position as a trainee manager with Bejam frozen food stores (now Iceland) and was soon in sole charge at a store in Eltham.

Then the Dodds curse struck again just as everything seemed to be going so well. This time it was through John. One day when he and Phyllis were out driving in the countryside, he felt unwell, drew into a lay-by and blacked out. Phyllis had to call an ambulance, and although John quickly recovered, with no apparent after-effects, follow-up examinations over a lengthy period revealed that he had an inoperable brain tumour.

The medical authorities could not be specific about how long John could live. It depended on whether they could prevent the tumour from developing but said it could be anything between four months and four years.

This was somewhere around 1973. The drugs seemed to be keeping the tumour under control for a long time and John continued his career. He was not told the seriousness of his condition and carried on a normal life. Phyllis made other moves in this period within the press and publicity area, and moved to a higher managerial grade at Liverpool Street. After a few years John was having blackouts, which became more and more frequent. To enable Phyllis to carry on working, Margaret helped her look after John when his condition worsened to the point where he had to give up work. It was not long before John needed constant professional nursing, and he was moved to a nearby hospice where he died on 16 March 1982 at the age of thirty-one. Phyllis was still only twenty-eight years old.

Phyllis was very bitter for a long time, and who could blame her? John was such a quiet, easygoing lad who would not have hurt a fly. The two of them had been enjoying a nice life, both with good jobs, and they enjoyed travelling on exotic holidays, which they did quite a lot. When Phyllis learned about the seriousness of John's condition she organised even more foreign trips for his benefit. They were very devoted to one another.

Fortunately, Phyllis had a big circle of friends among her many work colleagues, and they rallied round and tried to ease her pain. She devoted herself to her job, which she loved and was very good at, and this also helped to reduce her pain. Neither Phyllis nor I could ever understand why so many evil people can survive and flourish while harmless individuals like John Cooper are taken from their loved ones. It is a cruel world we live in.

My district had the biggest membership of all within the Union, around 15,000, when the average was not more than 10,000. The membership contained a good mixture, including initially some

London Transport members, ferry shore staff, and a considerable number of workshop staff at Ashford, Dartford, Croydon and Wimbledon. It was a very busy district but I enjoyed it like that.

Now and again, as I was in the London area, Head Office would call on me to take a meeting at national level in London. This was all good experience, because I was well placed geographically to pursue a position as Headquarters Officer and hopefully then Assistant General Secretary (AGS).

In fact around 1971 there was an election for AGS and I was encouraged to allow myself to be nominated for it. I thought it was too soon after my election as an organiser, but it was explained that if I got sufficient nominations, I would be allowed to take the examination which, as with the election for organiser, was necessary to be eligible for the ballot. The content of the examination was different from that for organiser. Once you had passed you automatically were included in future elections as long as you had the requisite number of nominations. I passed the exam, with a number of my colleagues, and received a respectable vote, coming about third out of six or seven.

I soldiered on contentedly, my members knowing that they had a potential AGS as their organiser. Then, early in 1975, when Sidney Greene, the General Secretary, retired, another election for AGS took place, which I again entered. I still only reached third place, but as a result of the then Headquarters Officer being elected AGS, his position became vacant. That position was an appointment of the Senior Organiser who was prepared to take the position.

Owing to the difficulty and cost of accommodation in the London area, it was not an attractive prospect for many of the provincial organisers, as the salary difference was only about ten per cent greater to compensate for deputising for any of the Assistant General Secretaries. In practice, that is what the position was – assistant to the Assistants. Although I was not the most senior of all the organisers, I was the senior of those willing to take the position. For me it was easy, as I was already resident in the London area, so there was no additional expense involved. The other attraction was that although the AGS was elected, it was always from among the Headquarters Officers.

Sidney Weighell became General Secretary in February 1975, and because of consequential upward moves, I was transferred to the Headquarters Officer's position at the same time. The Assistants whom I would be working with were Russell Tuck, Senior Assistant, Frank Cannon and Charles Turnock. I knew them all well as we had all been district organisers at one time, and looked forward to this new role.

The Senior Assistant was also a member of the Labour Party National Executive, and therefore either one of the other Assistants or myself covered his meetings with BR. There was also an involvement with London Transport engineering staff, who had a negotiating body jointly with the Engineering Unions, and I was the Joint Secretary of that body.

Jimmy Knapp had been elected as an organiser around 1970 when the Union decided to have an additional organiser exclusively for London Transport staff other than workshop staff. He had been branch secretary at the Kilmarnock and Hurlford branch.

When I became an organiser my branch at Harrow had closed and I decided to transfer my membership back to Kilmarnock and Hurlford, where I had come from. Jimmy Knapp had been the branch secretary in my first three or four years as an organiser. He had held that position at Kilmarnock and Hurlford since the time I had been in charge of the branch accounts section. I am sure he will well remember the preferential treatment he got as a branch secretary, through me, at that time a former member, being in charge of the section that dealt with all branch finances.

Our paths were destined to cross many times from then on, as it happened. When I got the appointment at Head Office, Jimmy's wife, Sylvia, who hailed originally from Folkestone, was keen for him to take up my district. If you have ambitions for the future, being resident in the London area is a big asset. Jimmy was the Officer who took over as District Officer in London South when I left. In fact he was transferred for a couple of weeks before I took up my position to enable me to introduce him around the district.

Shortly after Sid Weighell became General Secretary, the Union bought a country mansion at Frant, near Tunbridge Wells, which became a residential training college for members, particularly branch secretaries, who all attended (even before then) a week's training.

Three or four of the organisers were called on to help provide the training, Jimmy being one of them. This was something Sid Weighell had advocated before he became GS and carried it through soon after his election. It proved a great success, much to his credit, even though it was expensive to run. The Union was among the most affluent Unions in those days, having assets of around £15 million.

Chapter Six

I was thoroughly enjoying my new position, engaged in national negotiations for various grades of our members. One of my functions was to act as host when we had foreign visitors, which happened at least once every year. A programme of visits to various parts of the country was arranged, and wherever they stayed I did too. Shortly after I took up my new position we had a delegation from what was then East Germany. Within a few days a party arrived from the then Soviet Union. I escorted both groups for the rest of their stay, usually about ten days. This was a really interesting time. I had visitors from Canada, Romania, Japan, East Germany, Italy, Scandinavia, France, Austria and Belgium during my period as HQ Officer.

I think the highlight was with the Japanese visitors, whose main request was that the itinerary should include a game of golf at St Andrews. They were fanatical about golf, and especially about Scotland as the home of it. I had taken some lessons while an organiser and had been a midweek member at the famous Selsdon Park, so getting to play at St Andrews was a real perk of the job. Margaret always got to meet the visitors, as there was usually a visit to a theatre included, and Margaret would join us on such an occasion. The foreign visitors usually extended an invite to me to visit their country with Margaret, but the Union's practice was that any visits abroad extended to us should be composed of an AGS together with one or two members of the Executive Committee. Sometimes wives were included, their transport costs being met by the husband. Headquarters Officers were never included. I didn't mind, as I was sure my turn would arrive when I became an Assistant General Secretary.

It the early part of 1977, Sid Weighell had been away with a bad back on a number of occasions, resulting from a car accident some years earlier in which his wife was killed. Towards the middle of that year, June to be exact, he told Russell Tuck, his

Deputy, that he had been advised to have some time away from work and have a period of intensive treatment to clear it up.

The General Secretary's decision meant that the Executive Committee, in accordance with the Constitution of the Union, appointed Mr Tuck as Acting General Secretary, Mr Cannon as Acting Senior Assistant (i.e. Deputy General Secretary) and then me as the third Acting Assistant General Secretary. This was the real big time, and right until then I didn't know the gulf that existed between me as Headquarters Officer and the permanent Assistants.

This decision was taken shortly before the Annual General Meeting (AGM) was due at Ayr, my home county. It meant that I would be there as Acting Assistant with a specific role to play in putting forward the Union's policy on AGM Resolutions that came within my sphere of influence. Not only that, I would be making my appearance close to where I had begun my Union activity at local level. I was very excited at the thought.

I thoroughly enjoyed those two weeks in the Town Hall at Ayr, a favourite venue for NUR Annual General Meetings. Nobody will ever tell you on your initiation whether you have done well or not, but you will soon hear loud and clear if you make a mess of things. The fact that I didn't get that kind of reaction suggests I did okay.

My stint as Acting AGS lasted until December, six months in all, and was a great experience. Although passing the written examination is a step forward, there is no substitute for the real thing. I was well and truly ready for when my opportunity came.

The Union went through regular periods of crisis, including during my time as Headquarters Officer, as it had always done. However, as Headquarters Officer you were a step removed from the real nitty-gritty. I wasn't a member of the EC as Headquarters Officer. The General Secretary and his three Assistants were, and that is where the cut and thrust took place.

Sid Weighell had a very different style from that of Sidney Greene, his predecessor. That is not a criticism, it is merely a fact. Sidney Greene had been General Secretary since the fifties, with nearly eighteen years in the top position. In the Trade Union world he was among the most senior, and had been knighted and later made Lord Greene by the Wilson government. The respect he had in the wider movement prevailed on the NUR Executive Committee. Sid Weighell, although having had many years as the Deputy, still had to make his mark as General Secretary. He shared the same hatred of extreme political right-wingers and left-wingers as did Sid Greene, but he was less subtle than Sid Greene in handling them. It is true to say that there were never any extreme political right-wingers on the Executive.

The NUR Executive nearly always had around seven or eight Communists among its members. They did not hide their political affiliation, and in the main were very loyal to the Union. However, the time of Sid Weighell's election as General Secretary happened at about the same time that the Union appeared to be targeted by the Militant Tendency as ripe for infiltration. I am sure that the timing was no accident. A major change in leadership presents an ideal opportunity. You could recognise elements of it within the branches, but more so at grades conferences and in district councils. The NUR, like many other organisations, not just Trade Unions, suffer from apathy. That creates the ideal breeding ground for the anarchist types like the Militant Tendency.

The infiltration was not confined to the branches, district councils and grades conferences. There was some evidence that there were Militant supporters, if not members, among the Head Office staff as well.

Sid Weighell had recognised the disease before he became GS and had made clear his determination to eradicate it. That made him a lot of enemies, because the one thing the Tendency depended on was a type of intimidation whereby although not agreeing with their philosophy, so long as you did not formally oppose them, they would quietly expand their influence to a point where they could take over completely. Sid Weighell was standing in their way and it was bound to cause a clash. One-third of the Executive Committee retired each year, therefore by the beginning of 1978 there was a completely new Executive Committee from that which was in office when he was elected in 1975. It is also true that there was a fair proportion of extremely active Militant supporters among their number, even if they were not full-blown Militant members.

Sid Weighell decided to throw the book (the full NUR Constitution as contained within the *Union Rule Book*) at them. I fully supported his objectives, but I disagreed with the way he handled his attack on them. Using the Constitution is the correct method in normal circumstances, but these were not normal circumstances. It made Sid look 'too clever by half', a situation which attracted sympathy for those being attacked from among ordinary members who normally had no axe to grind. Militant members are also anarchists who have no respect for rule books, and will only squeal when they suffer through the use of their own methods. As I have stated earlier, their influence increases if they can lay claim to being persecuted.

That is how they presented the constitutional case Sid Weighell made against them. The loyalty to the General Secretary among sections of his staff was so suspect that he had to install a paper shredder in his private office to prevent leaks of sensitive material being produced to combat Militant.

Documents setting out how certain individuals were offending against the Constitution had to be produced in Head Office, so it was invaluable to have supporters there who could leak material to those being charged with such offences. That is why I would have chosen a different method for dealing with this difficulty. I am aware that hindsight is a skill that doesn't really exist, and it is always easier to operate from the sidelines. I held the same view at the time, but as Headquarters Officer I was not close enough to the General Secretary to have any influence on his decisions. There were some of my colleagues who were close enough to him to influence him, but they appeared to agree with his way of handling the problem. No doubt we all like to hear it said that what we are doing is right, when a word of caution would be much more effective.

The atmosphere between the GS and his executive got worse and worse to the point where even the majority who supported Sid began to wane. In his battle with the Militant supporters on the EC, the General Secretary began to withhold documents from them until the last possible minute before Executive meetings in an effort to prevent the material getting into the wrong hands outside the Union. That strategy offended the General Secretary's allies who were suffering as much as those in the line of attack.

Militant members and supporters infiltrated Sidney Weighell's 'baby', Frant Place, the training college, by getting selected as tutors from each district council area to fulfil that role in the training of workplace representatives, which was undertaken on an increasing scale at Frant. It must have been like a gift from heaven for Militant – their own formal breeding ground, and getting paid for it as well! It is little wonder that the situation was becoming extremely difficult.

The problems the NUR was experiencing through Militant infiltration was common among other Unions, particularly many of the white-collar Unions like the Teaching Unions, the Civil Service Unions, as well as most of the Manual Unions. They all seemed to have different methods of dealing with it. In fact some ignored it, which did not help those like the NUR who decided to combat it. Even the Labour Party administration staff had been infiltrated to a point where the National Executive Committee were spending more time and resources on dealing with staff problems than they were in preparing to govern the country.

I think the predecessor of Larry Whitty (the former General Secretary of the Labour Party) bore some responsibility for the grip Militant were able to gain at Walworth Road. There is no doubt that Militant had supporters within the National Executive in the late seventies and into the early eighties. In fact their influence may still exist through some current members of the Labour Party National Executive, even if the parent seems to have expired. It is true that in the main they have been weeded out since the Labour Party cleansed itself over recent years.

The same cannot be said of the Unions, particularly the Rail, Maritime and Transport Workers' Union (formerly the NUR). Sid Weighell gained some minor successes against them, but without the wholehearted support of the Executive Committee and the governing body of the Union, the Annual General Meeting, he was doomed to failure – so strong was their grip at all levels of the Union's structure. Many industrial disputes arose where it was obvious they were at the heart of the mischief. One such serious dispute concerned 'Flexible Rostering' for railway guards and footplate staff. It was aimed at securing increases in basic pay rates rather than relying on allowances which had no guarantees and which only a minority of staff received.

Another of Sidney Weighell's achievements was the establishment of the ASLEF/NUR Federation, a loose joint body of the respective Executives which met every few months to resolve difficulties and try to formulate common policies for improving conditions of service for traincrews. Len Murray (now Lord Murray) played a big part in giving birth to that body, with Sidney Weighell and Ray Buckton, a former ASLEF General Secretary.

It arose out of continual complaints to the TUC, mainly by the NUR, about ASLEF poaching members contrary to the principles of the Bridlington Agreement. This was a TUC agreement by Unions, whereby formal requests from the parent Union had to be made and agreed to before any transfer of members from one Union to another took place.

Essentially, it was a move towards the establishment of a single Rail Union, which had defied generations for one hundred years; therefore it was seen as a major breakthrough. Sid Weighell was a former footplate man, as was his Deputy, Russell Tuck, myself and at least six of the fifteen Divisional Officers. With that background we could all see the benefits which could be brought about. To give Ray Buckton his dues he was a willing participant in this exercise, even if the same could not be said for all his Executive Committee.

It was always accepted that it would take a long time to bring the exercise to a conclusion, but to grasp the nettle was a considerable move in the right direction. There seemed a number of non-controversial operations both Unions were performing separately which could be performed jointly with considerable financial savings all around. These were objectives that the Unions were encouraged by the TUC to embark on before trying to tackle the big problem. Some mutual benefit at that level would encourage further steps.

While the work situation continued at a fairly hectic pace, the domestic scene was not at a standstill. Around the time that Phyllis's husband, John, had his serious tumour diagnosed, with the outcome already described, Margaret's mother had what appeared to be a very small lump on the side of her knee. Within a few months it became as big as an egg, and when tests and examinations were carried out it too was diagnosed as a tumour.

Margaret and I had been in hospital for various major operations. Mine was for my old complaint of stomach ulcers. I made a complete and quick recovery within three months. Almost as soon as I came out of hospital, Margaret, who had not been well for some time, went in after they discovered she had a large growth internally. Fortunately it was not malignant and was removed successfully. However, in removing it, they damaged a kidney which failed. To repair the failure meant another major operation within a week of the first one. Again this was carried out successfully. It was only after Margaret began to make a recovery that we realised how near to death she had been. The doctor who discovered the problem (not our regular one) said that if she had not got Margaret to hospital that day she would have died. This time we escaped...

This was all happening in the few years around 1976–78. In fact Alison got married when Margaret was in hospital, therefore that was a wedding in the family that Margaret never got to attend.

After Margaret's mother underwent an operation to remove the tumour from her leg, she had to attend hospital daily, travelling over forty miles from home by taxi at her own expense to have radiotherapy treatment. When you think of that situation about twenty years ago involving a woman aged over seventy, during the lifetime of a Labour Government, it makes you realise how long the NHS has been in turmoil. The nearest place able to provide the treatment, a few minutes of it, was nearly fifty miles away. They would have had her as an in-patient, but to try and avoid that the alternative was treatment as an outpatient at her own transport cost. I think it was just as disgusting then as some of the shortcomings are now.

The outcome of the treatment left my mother-in-law with a large open raw wound about three inches across and seven or eight inches long. It needed daily dressing by the nurse, sometimes twice daily. I don't know how Margaret's father and mother coped with it, but they did, and still came and spent time with us on a regular basis. They certainly bred them tough in those days. We had been having our full share of family health problems in those few years. The Dodds curse could not be blamed for all of this, as it was now reaching those connected to the Dodds family: John Cooper, Margaret and her mother as well as me.

Among the many family events, most of which were not of the joyous kind, there was the odd happening which did bring us great joy. One such occurred on 4 May 1981 when my daughter Alison gave birth to our first grandchild, Daniel. He seemed a very healthy baby at first and of course Margaret and I were over the moon. We would have liked a son of our own as well as our two lovely daughters, but it was not to be. Getting a grandson as our first grandchild was the next best thing.

It was not long after Daniel's birth that it was discovered he had a serious food allergy. He was allergic to almost everything other than his mother's milk. He had to be fed thereafter on a special powdered non-dairy type of milk which came from the USA. Fortunately he thrived on it, but his allergy lasted for many years. When he became a toddler it was very difficult and he found it strange because he could not have the things most children enjoy, such as sweets, ice cream and the like. His treats were a packet of potato crisps, and the only sweets that did not upset him were the occasional packet of Polo mints. He was in and out of Great Ormond Street Children's Hospital regularly, with a view to finding a cure. In the end it was only by trial and error that he began to eat some normal food. One of his treats at that time that Margaret provided was a piece of dry white bread. He ate that in the same way a normal child ate a piece of cake or a fancy biscuit.

Gradually, bit by bit, he became able to eat normally, but that was after he was around eight years old. Now that he's between fifteen and sixteen years old you can't find enough junk food to satisfy him, and he is nearly six feet tall. We often think that although it was a difficult period, he did miss all the earlier junk food, and certainly didn't ruin his teeth on sweets. We are so proud of Daniel, having come through this early difficult time.

Most of my time as Headquarters Officer was spent assisting AGS Frank Cannon. He dealt with BR engineering staff, British Transport Docks staff and all the Hotel and Catering workers.

British Transport Docks Board operated a job evaluation scheme for their workers, and we had most of the crane drivers and checkers as members of the NUR. They were very key grades in the ports, and nothing moved if the crane drivers were in dispute. Stoppages in that grade, particularly at Southampton, were not uncommon, and therefore keeping the peace and administering the job evaluation scheme was a time-consuming job.

Frank Cannon was what could be described in Trade Union jargon as 'a wily old bird'. I loved working with and for Frank, because he taught you every trick in the trade, and he and I seemed to have a mutually good relationship.

I always remember an occasion early in my period at Head Office when I had been in Frank's office bringing him up to date with particular problems he had delegated to me. I must have come from Frank's room looking very pleased, because Barry Kew, an administration officer then and a good friend as well, said, 'You look well pleased with yourself, Andy. What have you been up to?'

I told him what I had reported to Frank, and he asked me what Frank's reaction was. I said he was well pleased and had said, 'You are doing a good job there, I'm glad I asked you to do that.'

Barry said, 'I should tell you, Andy, that Frank's responses don't always mean what they appear to mean. In fact, we have a list in our room of Frank's sayings and what they actually mean, and his response to you that you were doing a good job and "I'm glad I gave it to you to do for me", actually means "F— off, can't you see I'm busy!"' I thought that was hilarious, and of course he threw managements off guard with a similar approach. They never knew whether he was serious or not. Another of his gifted quotations was, 'Confidence is the feeling you had before you understood the problem.'

78

Frank was grooming me to succeed him as an AGS. He did not enjoy the best of health, and continually let me know he would be retiring very shortly. There was no better tutor in the skills of negotiation than Frank Cannon. He would have made a top-class barrister. His qualities were recognised by all the employers he dealt with, and he was very popular with the members he represented as well. To have respect on as broad a front as that is no mean achievement.

I still did some work for Russell Tuck and to a lesser extent for Charles Turnock too. Most of my time was in Frank's area as, when Russell needed cover, Frank provided it.

Russell Tuck was the Senior Assistant General Secretary (Deputy General Secretary) and I had known him from before I came to work for the Union in 1960. Before he was elected an Officer he was a tutor at the NUR residential schools in the late 1950s. In the second half of 1959 I had attended an NUR school at a training college in Chester-le-Street, Co. Durham. Russell was one of the tutors at that school. Among the students were quite a few who like myself became Officers or members of the Executive Committee. Becoming a National Officer under Russell was in many ways a great tribute to his teaching from the earlier years. As Senior AGS he dealt only with BR matters in negotiation, and there were lower areas of his responsibility that were mine directly. The Senior Assistant by tradition had always been elected to the Labour Party National Executive, and that took up a lot of time. This was part of the reason the Union decided to elect a third Assistant in the late 1970s. We enjoyed a good relationship; no doubt the student and tutor relationship of some seventeen years earlier made that easy.

I had attended a number of residential schools throughout the 1950s. One was in London, organised by the TUC, and one was near Sheffield at Wortley Hall, organised by the Labour Party. I also did a number of correspondence courses through the National Council of Labour Colleges. I suppose in hindsight that those activities did a lot in preparing me for the role I was involved in at this time. I confess I had no plans for a career in the Trade Union when I was doing the courses. Charles Turnock, whom I only knew from the time I became a divisional organiser

– as was the case with Frank Cannon – was another senior colleague whom I had good relations with. I did less deputising for Charles than the others, though.

Being Headquarters Officer and deputising for the three Assistants with the various employers was a marvellous experience. It was the ultimate training ground, and after a few years I was ready and capable of fulfilling any role within the Union.

Even before being appointed to that position in 1975, I was attending the training establishments of employers as well as the Union, not as a student but as a guest contributor.

BR was the principal partner in the British Transport Staff College at Woking, which was in my area when I was a Divisional Officer, and they ran three-month courses for senior managers. I attended every one of those courses as a guest contributor, and on a separate day during the same course arranged to be able to take a group of local workplace representatives there as well. My local representatives loved that occasion, and to their credit they always gave a good display of their ability.

Early in 1980 Frank Cannon made it known to me that he would be intimating to the General Secretary that he wanted to retire at the end of the year. As I had already passed the AGS examination, I could begin campaigning with the confidence of knowing I would be in the ballot. However, by this time a second Headquarters Officer position had been created, to which another of the London Divisional Organisers had been appointed, who like myself had also passed the examination for AGS. This was Brian Arundel, and he was closer to Charles Turnock and Sidney Weighell than I was. Charles, although the junior of the three Assistants, was an extremely close confidant of the General Secretary, and when the vacancy for an Assistant was officially announced, Brian became a candidate with the support of Charles and to some extent that of the General Secretary, albeit a little less openly. It has to be borne in mind up until this time although those positions were open to all, the holder of the most senior position had always succeeded to the next level. Brian and I were holding equal positions, but I had been appointed some years earlier and would normally have been supported by my senior colleagues.

Two of the other divisional organisers, Jimmy Knapp and Vernon Hince, had also been nominated, but they had yet to pass the test, and in times past they would not have been a threat even if they passed the examination. When Jimmy Knapp took over my division in 1975, as I explained, he was heavily involved in the training of branch secretaries and other workplace representatives at Frant House, which was now paying off in the high number of nominations for Assistant he received from branches the length and breadth of the country. He had twice as many nominations than me, although on past practice I would have been a clear favourite. I still had one advantage: I had passed the examination, whereas Jimmy still had that hurdle to cross. Those of us who had become Divisional Officers usually passed the AGS examination. Jimmy and Vernon both failed the examination, to the surprise of a great number of people, and therefore would not be in the ballot.

There were some suggestions afterwards that the test papers and answers had been tampered with before the test, and that a fresh set of papers were substituted the morning of the examination. I have no idea whether or not there was any truth in that story, but the fact that Brian and I were left to fight this election on our own completely altered the situation, which had been running very heavily in Jimmy Knapp's favour up until then.

Despite apparently not being the favoured candidate of certainly Charles Turnock, nor probably the General Secretary, I had a big lead in nominations over Brian.

That lead in nominations I had over Brian was transformed into votes in my favour. At a Special Meeting early in October 1981, the result of the election was declared:

| Arundel | 44,099 |
| Dodds | 100,497 |

There was a membership of around 200,000 at this time, and branches voted as a block vote. Over one hundred branches did not record votes at all.

I was very proud of this huge victory over my only opponent. The past traditions of the NUR had held firm this time, even though there were strong indications at one stage of the campaign that those traditions were going to be laid aside. In normal circumstances, I would not complain if the traditions of the past had not held up. After all, I had been in earlier elections for Assistant General Secretary, opposing senior colleagues, because I felt I could do the job as well as them, if not better.

However in this election, where I had succeeded, the influence of Militant was very much in evidence, and they were not supporting me or Brian Arundel.

It appeared that the traditions of the past, so far as elections to senior positions were concerned, would not last much longer. As I have said earlier, this would not bother me as long as it produced the best person for the job, but there was no guarantee that when the traditions did break down, that would actually be the case. I had always felt wherever I had worked that I wanted to succeed on my ability rather than by seniority.

The Executive Committee appointed me to commence duties a few weeks after the election result was declared. Meanwhile my position as one of two Headquarters Officers had to be filled by the Senior DO wishing to take the position. As often was the case, this fell to a London-based DO and again it was to be Jimmy Knapp who followed in my footsteps. Once more I was to spend a few weeks showing Jimmy the duties he would be covering. Charles Turnock would move to take over the sphere of influence that Frank Cannon was leaving, while I would take over the duties of Charles Turnock. As there were now two Headquarters Officers, Jimmy Knapp would mainly be working under me, while Brian Arundel would be assisting Russell Tuck and his friend, Charles Turnock.

My area of responsibility was to be docks, hotel, train and station catering, Sealink, goods and cartage members, together with bus members and London Transport at national negotiating level. I also was responsible for railway regional negotiating for Western and Scottish regions. In addition I would represent the Union on a number of international committees, particularly road haulage and food workers. I was also appointed to be a member of the National Dock Labour Board. This was a statutory body and I was appointed by the Minister of Labour following nomination by the TUC. I had held an appointment as a member of the industrial tribunals for a number of years as a Divisional Officer and as Headquarters Officer, which was also an appointment from the Minister of Labour following nomination by the TUC.

Having such great responsibilities as I have outlined was certainly going to be a big challenge but I was looking forward to this with great confidence. I had a potential ten years of service to prove myself as one of the four Senior Officers.

I was very excited by what lay before me over the next decade. Many of my predecessors had reached this level long before the age of fifty-five, which I was. However, few were better equipped, because only one had the administration experience I had gained in my six and a half years as a member of the staff; this had been followed by nine years as a Divisional Organiser and a further six and a half years as Headquarters Officer.

When I came back to Head Office in 1975, many of the staff I had worked alongside as a member of the staff between 1960 and 1966 were themselves managers of departments. I had no difficulty in my new role than compared to most of them, but there were one or two who could not hide their dislike of the situation. Fortunately the majority were as proud of the door I had opened by being elected a Divisional Officer from the staff as I was. In fact my good friend, Len Bound, had followed me a few years later by also being elected a Divisional Officer. Before I retired in 1991, two more young members of the staff also got elected. They were Peter King and Lawrence Cramer, both good friends of mine, who acknowledged the help and encouragement I gave them in pursuing the same goal. They might even go the whole way instead of stumbling at the final hurdle as I did. That part of the story is still to come.

The Union was facing one of those major critical periods around the time I took over my duties. For a long time a reorganisation of traincrews' (drivers' and guards') rosters had been taking place, referred to as 'Flexible Rostering'. It had been a long exercise but just before Christmas 1981 final proposals were put to the two Unions. There were deep divisions within the

Executive Committee of both Unions regarding the proposals because it was seen as the end of guaranteed working times.

This was one of the occasions where the influence of Militant was showing within the NUR Executive even if that was not the reason for the division on the ASLEF Executive Committee. Just before the NUR Executive were due to vote on whether to accept the proposals or not, I remember being present at a meeting of the NUR Executive's Negotiating Committee when a well-known EC member and an ardent member of the Communist Party, Jock Nicholson, wiped the floor (by argument) in favour of the proposals with another guard member of the EC from Merseyside (the home of Militant) named Ian Williams. The gist of Jock's argument to Williams was that he was simply opposing support for the proposals without being able to explain what his opposition was. There was some money being withheld by the BR pending agreement being reached. With only days to go before the deadline, the NUR accepted the proposals, thereby releasing this money. Ray Buckton of ASLEF and his negotiating team had accepted the proposals at their final meeting with BR; but whereas Sid Weighell had managed to persuade his EC to accept them, Ray Buckton was not able to get the backing of his EC.

The year 1981 ended with a deep division between the two Unions, not an uncommon occurrence, but one that was now tearing them both apart. Early in 1982, ASLEF went on strike on the issue and I saw the spectacle of members of the NUR Executive taking a collection among themselves to hand to ASLEF to show their support for the stand ASLEF were taking. It was a bizarre situation, when you remember the NUR had supported the proposals. It was clear that the Militant influence was again playing a big part in this inter-Union rivalry.

The first year after my election, i.e. 1982, is dealt with very fully in the General Secretary Sidney Weighell's book, *On the Rails* published by Ortis Publishing Ltd after his resignation at the end of 1982. Therefore I will confine my remarks to some of the events where I differ from Sidney's view.

I have already said I agreed that there was an attack being made on Sid by Militant. I repeat my view that I think his method of dealing with this problem was not the most productive and that he was being badly advised. They achieved their objective and brought him down. Not only that; they replaced him with someone who they considered would be less troublesome to the growth of their influence within the NUR.

Although I am not mentioned in Sidney Weighell's book, I was in the delegation at the 1982 Labour Party Conference in Blackpool that led to Sid's resignation later that year. The delegation comprised the elected members from the EC Districts, plus the President (Tommy Ham from Derby on that occasion), two of his three Assistants and his Private Secretary (Bill Little). Russell Tuck, his Deputy, was the other Assistant in the delegation besides myself. Russell was on the Party National Executive and as a senior member of it had a full role to play at the Conference on behalf of the Party.

The voting for the National Executive was always decided by our Executive Committee before the conference, and the practice was for the General Secretary to physically complete the voting paper in accordance with the EC's decision. Among their candidates for support on the Trade Union section was the Miners' Union nominee, Eric Clarke. Voting then was not as open as it is now.

There was reason to believe that the miners had not been supporting our nominee, Russell Tuck. Sid wrote to Arthur Scargill, the miners' President, seeking an assurance that they would support our nominee. He had not had a reply by the time Conference took place, and he took it upon himself not to deliver our vote for Eric Clarke. Horse-trading in votes was commonplace in that period. I am not trying to defend Sid's action, merely putting the whole picture forward. When it was discovered what had happened, Sid never returned to the conference, effectively leaving me with the President, in charge of the delegation, who were, by a heavy majority, against Sid Weighell. It was the first time I had been at the Labour Party Conference as a delegate, and here I was in charge of the delegation from our Union. What a daunting baptism that proved to be!

The delegates have a very restricted role in that the EC take decisions on what items we will support or oppose, and they only have freedom to decide on a few issues where we have no clear policy. The same is true of their intention to speak on issues before the conference; they must have the permission of the General Secretary or President. It has to be borne in mind that many of the delegates held personal views in direct opposition to that which they were being instructed to support. What view they held depended on which faction within the Labour Party they were in. It is sufficient to say that there was a strong *Hard Left* view prevailing among the majority of our delegation.

I certainly had a rough couple of days trying to hold the delegation together until we got back to London. I had always had a high regard for Sidney Weighell, as I had for whoever was General Secretary, but I have to say in those couple of days that loyalty was severely stretched. I would not wish my worst enemy to go through an experience of that kind.

The year 1982 ended with a campaign for Sidney Weighell's successor following the failed attempt to get the Special General Meeting at Birmingham to allow Sid to reconsider his decision. Although Sid Weighell makes it clear in his book, *On the Rails*, that he favoured Charles Turnock to take his place, that would have been in line with tradition; and although I would have run against him as he had run against Sid Weighell, I would not have any objections to Charles being elected. Sid does not disclose in his book, however, the meetings he and Charles and I had at a secret location outside London with the President to try and arrive at a strategy to prevent Jimmy Knapp being elected General Secretary.

At one stage Sid suggested that because Charles was the same age as him, i.e. with only about three or four years to retirement, whereas I still had nine years to go, it might be in the best interests of trying to keep Jimmy from being elected if I was to stand as the only Assistant with the support of the others. Russell was not considered as he had intimated his decision to retire too. Sid's suggestion fell on stony ground as far as Charles was concerned.

This was the one position where the candidates did not have to pass an examination before entering the ballot. The architects of the Constitution, when the Union was formed more than seventy years earlier, held the view that the General Secretary was more likely than not to come from among the Assistants and would therefore have already passed an examination. Jimmy Knapp's high number of nominations when he failed the Assistant's exam in 1981 was a clear indication that there was a strong band of opinion behind him, despite his inexperience at a senior level; in fact, the organised Hard Left supporting him probably felt someone with little experience at that level would be an advantage to them. I believe time has proved that view to be correct. The Hard Left supporters who elected Jimmy have run roughshod over the Constitution during his tenure.

Early in 1983 the election for Sidney Weighell's successor got under way. The nominees were, as expected, Charles Turnock, myself, Jimmy Knapp and my good friend, Benny Entwistle, the Divisional Officer from the Manchester area. We were the only ones with the requisite number of nominations. No examinations were necessary, although Benny Entwistle, like many of the DOs, had sat and passed the AGS examination a number of years earlier – in fact, before me, as he had been an Officer before me as well.

The campaign ran for around ten weeks, and as was anticipated there was massive support being shown by way of nominations for Jimmy Knapp. Charles and myself, having been two of Sid Weighell's Assistants, were finding we were not getting the support we expected, mainly on the grounds of having been too close to Sid, although it could have been argued that with just about four years to serve Charles had an extra disadvantage. Although I had over nine to serve, and until then appeared to have fulfilled my duties satisfactorily, I was faring even worse than Charlie. The outcome seemed weighted heavily in favour of Jimmy Knapp, and this is the message we were getting in attending meetings up and down the country. The rank and file members attending those meetings left me in no doubt that whereas in the past, experience at all the lower levels was a deciding factor, this was not going to be the case this time.

The Militant Tendency had infiltrated the NUR in a big way around the time of Sid Weighell's election as General Secretary early in 1975. There were lots of signs regarding this during those years, and Jimmy Knapp became their tool as a National Officer when he became Headquarters Officer in 1981 following my election as an Assistant General Secretary. In fact, judging by the number of nominations Jimmy Knapp received in that election, it is almost certain he would have defeated me for that position. It was only his inability to pass the Assistant's examination to gain access to the ballot which enabled me to succeed.

Following Jimmy's election as a Divisional Officer in 1970, he and I had an understanding. This was necessary as we were both from the same branch, and only one of us could be nominated for Officer elections within the rules. When I had been on the administration staff and Jimmy had been branch secretary at Hurlford and Kilmarnock, he was in some difficulty with the affairs of the branch. I was aware of this and alerted local colleagues to have the matter put right. Jimmy had indicated following his becoming an Officer that he would not oppose me in future elections, being sufficiently younger to almost guarantee his future as leader following my retirement. He did not keep his word on that understanding, allowing himself to become the tool of Militant and the Hard Left.

It had always been the case in the past that General Secretaries came from the Assistants, usually the Senior Assistant. As Sid Weighell, Russell Tuck and Charles Turnock were almost exactly the same age, a problem was always on the cards unless Sid had retired at age sixty. Even then Russell or Charles would not have been expected to run for General Secretary. I would have been the natural choice, but Sid and Charles had been pushing for Brian Arundel, my junior.

The Hard Left were cleverer than their opponents when it came to strategy. They never allowed individuals to thwart the movement's objectives, unlike the moderates. Charles had no chance of being elected General Secretary in 1983 because of his age. Years earlier that should have been recognised, together with the attack being mounted on the moderate leadership by Militant and the Hard Left, and a campaign should have been mounted behind me, including Jimmy Knapp. Because of the obligation Jimmy had to me, if he had been faced with it, I believe he would have delivered on his earlier understanding with me. I never revealed before now to anyone about our understanding or the reasons for it. That was never my style. In fact, from what I had seen of previous General Secretaries, you needed to be devious. I never was, and could not have become so. If that was needed to succeed, I am glad I didn't win.

The result, which came towards the end of February, was almost a humiliation as far as Charles and myself were concerned. Jimmy Knapp received over 90,000 votes, Charles Turnock just over 35,000, and me a derisory 11,000. Benny Entwistle, in most members' view an exemplary Officer, got only just over 6,000 votes. The NUR now had the least experienced General Secretary in its history. Is that what the Hard Left wanted?

I think they did. That achievement allowed them to continue their rampage from a position of strength. They were an anarchist organisation, making the rules to suit their purposes.

Russell Tuck, who had been Acting General Secretary since Sid Weighell's resignation in October, had intimated he would be retiring after the AGM in July. He stayed just long enough to introduce Jimmy to his new position. It was a difficult transition for all of us in these early months. Jimmy had been our junior since he filled the Headquarters Officer position when I was elected an Assistant just over a year earlier. Now all of a sudden we were his Assistants. I felt bad enough about the situation, but I knew it would be more difficult for Charles Turnock than for me, because he was about to become Jimmy's Deputy as soon as Russell went. He had had that very close relationship with Sid, so it was never going to be a happy situation. Previous General Secretaries and their Deputies had never had very close relationships; that was true of Sidney Greene and Sidney Weighell, and of Sidney Weighell and Russell Tuck, so this one would be even more difficult.

I decided that, as far as I was concerned, the members had made their decision and the Union was more important than any individual, therefore we had to get on with it. I told Jimmy that and he thanked me for it. He knew it was going to be a trying time, without anybody making it more difficult. On the face of it Charles got stuck in, although he had always been an individual who did not suffer fools gladly.

There were great problems for all Trade Unions at this time; the Tory Government were attacking us all with great vigour through their anti-Trade Union legislation, and they had just been re-elected for another five years. We had all hoped the Labour Party would win the election and call a halt to the attack on the Unions which Margaret Thatcher's Government had been making since her election in 1979. We had tremendous industrial problems in the rail industry, and we were soon to be in the thick of it.

Certainly, being elected AGS towards the end of 1981 could have been read as a sign that the tide was really turning in my favour. But little was I to know at that time what was going to strike us as a family over the next few years.

I have earlier referred to the sad death of Phyllis's husband, John, after a long struggle against the scourge of a brain tumour, and later of how Margaret's mother had been found also to have a nasty tumour on her leg. The fact that Margaret's parents were, by 1980, getting towards their eighties did not make it easier when we began to see them go downhill. Being four hundred miles away from them made it even more difficult when they began to falter. While for a number of years we were mainly concerned with Margaret's mother, who had been admirably nursed by her father, it was her father who was to die first. He had rapidly begun to go downhill, and he died very soon after being taken to hospital on 14 February 1983. That was a big blow, and a further strain on Margaret, who now had to cope with her mum being on her own – that is, without her dad. Margaret's brother, Drew, lived nearby, and while that was some comfort it was nothing like the attention Margaret would have provided. To Margaret's credit she made frequent visits to spend some time with her mother, and on a number of occasions we brought her down to us for some weeks.

We were only just into the third year of the decade and had already suffered two family deaths; not very good.

Phyllis concentrated on her career after John Cooper's death, and moved on promotion a few times between the Southern Region Press and Publicity Department and that of the Eastern Region at Liverpool Street. Phyllis had a wide circle of friends within the industry and outside it and they gave her great support through a difficult period.

I suppose it was quite unusual, if not unique, to have a father in a senior position in the Union of the industry where one is reaching senior levels in management. Not too many people at higher levels in the industry knew about the connection (although the then chairman of BR, Sir Peter Parker, was one who did); and although Phyllis was still a Union member, she was very loyal to her responsibilities as a member of a management team in a sensitive area such as Press and Public Affairs. Phyllis was good at her job, and that is the quality that was recognised by those who promoted her. As a female at her level in those days she was pioneering on behalf of other females for the future. BR was not any better in relation to the number of females in senior positions pro rata than any other of the large corporations.

Around the time of Jimmy Knapp's start as General Secretary we were soon involved with the miners' strike. Jimmy was obviously keen to rebuild the former strong bonds that had generally existed between our two Unions following the near-feuding that seemed to have taken place between Arthur Scargill and Sid Weighell. That meant we were soon heavily involved by refusing to move certain trains serving collieries and power stations. Those trains would be loading coal from the vast stocks that were on the surface at every colliery in the country – stocks so big they could have served power stations for the best part of a year. In fact it did not seem the best strategy for a strike to be called at the end of the winter, and when surface stocks were so high. I never regarded Arthur Scargill as the greatest Trade Union strategist, so maybe it proved my point.

It has to be remembered that the Thatcher Government had just been re-elected with a huge majority and had considerably toughened the already tough anti-Trade Union laws to a point where it was becoming virtually impossible to support another Union's dispute without facing penalties through the courts.

Injunctions could and were granted within hours, stopping secondary actions being taken, on peril of the Union's funds being confiscated. We were within an inch of that situation many times, because the Militant influence in our Union wanted to ignore these injunctions. 'Sacrifice' was all they shouted about – be seen to be making a sacrifice, no matter that it didn't do an iota to help those in a dispute, and in fact it would make their position weaker.

Despite all the difficulties, ways were found to make large payments in *hard cash*. Hundreds of thousands of pounds in total went to the Miners' Union and other Unions as well. So much of the Union's energy was spent during the early part of 1983 fighting our own severe problems and trying to support others.

When it came to other Unions seeking financial support, the NUR was seen as a soft touch. The Union has being paying the price for this generous aid over recent years and have themselves been in severe financial difficulties for some time now. Very few of these loans and donations, etc. were ever recovered, and that is one reason for the difficulty the Union has been experiencing. The other difficulty is having an oversized full-time Executive Committee, which costs around £1 million a year – an awful lot of contributions.

Still another part of the difficulty in finances was the high price we had to pay branch representatives to ensure members' votes were gathered in strike ballots. There was very little control over the number of days branches could claim against 'Loss of Worktime' in relation to strike ballots. Even though the legislation contained provision to claim from the Government for expenses incurred in strike ballots, our Militant friends wanted their hands kept clean on that issue by refusing to use the legislation where it could be in their favour. Talk about being politically correct – it was financial suicide.

We were under severe attack within our own industry too, because there were many in BR who were enjoying their new-found muscle and were continually flexing it. Massive reorganisation was taking place within each group of grades, and those exercises were very time-consuming. I often wonder if such tactics by employers, time-consuming working parties, etc., are in fact a blatant attempt at sapping the energy of the Unions with their limited resources.

With the retirement of Russell Tuck in the middle of 1983, I became the Number Two of the three Assistants, Vernon Hince being elected as the third Assistant. By this time examinations before ballots for Assistants had been dispensed with.

The three Assistants had set areas of responsibility for sections of the membership, and I moved from that of bus, London Transport, goods and cartage members to take over all BR engineering, British Transport Docks members, hotel and station catering and train catering. Additionally, each had responsibility for two BR regions as far as railway regional matters were concerned. Internally I had responsibility for legal matters and organisation matters.

Each of the three Assistants had a very full workload, the Senior Assistant dealing only with BR as an employer, partly because of the size of that section of the membership and also because the Senior Assistant was the Union's nominee to the Labour Party National Executive and historically was always elected. That responsibility took up probably as much as half of the workload, especially bearing in mind that Militants had infiltrated the Labour Party administration staff to a point where the National Executive were spending more than half their time dealing with staff problems. If it wasn't for the damage they did (which was their objective) you would have to admire how they could so embroil a governing body as to render it ineffective in its major role. It had to be seen to be believed! I am sure they must have taken lessons from Hitler's Fifth Column.

Charles Turnock, who was elected to the National Executive in Russell Tuck's place at the 1983 Party Conference and had the reputation for being a strong character, took on many of Russell's responsibilities in the Labour Party Organisation.

In my time as Headquarters Officer, from 1975 to 1981, part of my responsibility was playing host to foreign visitors. We usually had at least one such group every year, often more. In the first year, 1975, I was hosting delegations from the former East Germany and the Soviet Union. The practice was that the office would arrange the itinerary for the visit, usually around ten days, and would allocate one of the administration staff to accompany us. This was during the period of Sid Weighell's General Secretaryship, and he left me to carry out this function in a way I thought would suit our visitors. Although I had no experience of how best to organise the time outwith the formal itinerary, I felt at these times that it would be best if I devoted myself exclusively to our visitors. They were always based in a hotel in London like the Charing Cross or the Royal Great Western. On such occasions, although I only lived thirty minutes out of London, I stayed where they did, and on every occasion it seemed to work to our best advantage. The Soviets and the East Germans always had their own interpreter and that took care of the language difficulties. I never asked my predecessor, Charles Turnock, how he carried out those duties, but did it as I thought would benefit our guests. Obviously for me it was a *perk*, but to them it was important that in a short time they wanted to learn as much as they could from their trip. From reports I had afterwards, it seemed my attitude to this responsibility was well received. I later learned that Charles would bid them goodnight after dinner and meet them after breakfast next morning. I was with them twenty-four hours a day, and in the main they enjoyed that, because after the official day was over they could question me about various aspects of each day.

In my nearly seven years of carrying out this function, I hosted delegations from the Soviet Union, East Germany, Romania, Canada, Japan, Sweden, Denmark and Italy. I met a great number of interesting people during those visits, and came across a number of the colleagues in the delegations later in my role as an Assistant General Secretary. I found this responsibility to be of great interest and made many friends internationally as a result.

Obviously, international politics, particularly among the Soviet bloc, was at the forefront of their visits. All of those that I have referred to took place during the Cold War and were for other purposes than simply fostering international Trade Union links, so far as our friends from the Eastern bloc were concerned. Nevertheless, the contacts were valuable from our point of view too, even if it was only to emphasise the value of the freedom (restricted though it may have been under the Thatcher regime) we had in this country.

Among the delegations that we played host to who were less politically motivated than the Soviet bloc were the Japanese. It was usual in arranging an itinerary to ask visitors to tell us of anything in particular they would like included. When this question was posed to our Japanese friends, they indicated they would leave it to us with the proviso that their visit should include a visit to St Andrews in Scotland and a game of golf on the world-famous Old Course. That request was included as part of a visit to Springburn Works in Glasgow. I had played a little golf before going to HQ in 1975 and was as excited about the prospect as they were. One of the delegation left with thirty golf hats as souvenirs for his colleagues after playing on the Old Course and said he would be the envy of his friends.

Chapter Seven

While my career had been progressing over the last several years, so had Phyllis's. She had several promotions in the years since John died, mainly between Waterloo and Liverpool Street, and by early 1986 she was in Management Grade 3 – very high up for one so young, at only thirty-five. A remarkable girl and popular with it.

Although 1986 was another year of some tragedy in the family, it ended with a happy event. The tragedy, although it came as a blessing, was when Margaret's mother died towards the end of April. Margaret had been spending a lot of time in Scotland caring for her when it became difficult to bring her south. She had suffered terribly over ten years and was very brave. Margaret had done a marvellous job since her father died in looking after her mother, but ultimately she was suffering so much pain that it was a relief to everyone when the end came. I missed her greatly myself because, although in the early days of our marriage we were not very close, we grew to love each other very much, and there was nothing she would not do for me, the girls or Margaret. It was a heavy blow to Margaret, but because the suffering was over, that helped to dull the pain.

During the time Margaret was in Scotland with her mother, Phyllis had been going steady with Laurence from Otford. He had a travel agent's business in Biggin Hill, and she told us she was getting married to him in June. We were very happy about that, more so because that announcement came at the time that her grandma was nearing death. Phyllis and I had an arrangement, whereby if she came to move from her nice house in Orpington, she would offer it to me before it went on the market. She kept her promise, but as Margaret was preoccupied with her mother at the time, she was not so keen on it as me; but she let me go ahead with it on our joint behalf.

I am happy to say that after a short time in Orpington,

Margaret has not been happier in the four homes we have lived in since we came south.

Phyllis got married in June 1986, and it was a wonderful occasion for all of us. She sold her house to her mother and me, and Laurence, who already had a house in Otford, sold his as well, and they bought another in the village. We were all so happy, after the trauma of the previous few years, at seeing Phyllis settled again with a husband and this time planning to have a family. Little did we know then how short-lived that happiness was to be. That is for later, however.

Margaret and I prepared for this our fourth move since we left Scotland. Phyllis's house was in good order and, with a little decoration and some fitted bedroom furniture installed, we were able to move in in July 1986.

We had spent eighteen mainly happy years in Selsdon among nice friends we had made there, and left with a little sorrow, but as we were only moving eight miles further east we would still see them all from time to time. I was within five years of retirement; Alison was living in Chatham, and our move to Orpington meant the family were still relatively close together.

Alison had had domestic problems for a few years, which ended her marriage, but Phyllis did a great deal for her to keep us all together. We had a lot of bad times but we had pulled through and we seemed to be getting it behind us.

Phyllis's remarriage led to her first child being born on 28 March 1988 – a lovely girl named Elizabeth Louise Allen. After all Phyllis's earlier misfortunes, it seemed she had entered a new life. We were all so pleased. Within two years the event was repeated when Robert James was born on 1 December 1989. We were not to know then that this new-found happiness for Phyllis was to be short-lived.

Phyllis was considering ending her career on the railways at this stage and joining Laurence in the travel business which he was running, and which Phyllis had become a partner in. The railways were then preparing for privatisation, being split into operating units which would become Operating Companies. Her then boss, Jeff Harrison-Mees, was employing Phyllis on a casual basis to cover for staff on training courses. On one of those occasions he asked Phyllis to return full time as his Public Affairs Officer in an Executive Grade. At thirty-six years of age, this was a massive move upwards, and Phyllis accepted, returning to work full time, with Christine, who had been family nanny to Laurence and his younger brother, Clive, becoming nanny to Elizabeth and Robert.

I had become Senior Assistant (Deputy) General Secretary early in 1987, and Phyllis an Executive Grade Manager in the same industry in 1989. Alison took over the newspaper cutting service Phyllis had been operating at home for her division of the South-East, providing rail-related stories in the local papers of Kent and East Sussex. A high-powered railway organisation was being developed within our family. I am sure somebody would have had us investigated if they had realised the connection. Phyllis and Alison were both women of considerable resilience; there was no way they would not be good at whatever they chose to do for a career.

When I took on the responsibility for BR Engineering workers there was already a major rundown of that activity taking place. Ashford Works had been closed and many of the others were under threat of closure, the next in line being Shildon in Co. Durham, with its proud historic tradition going back to the early development of the railways. I had just returned from leading a delegation to the Soviet Union, which I will refer to later. This was the first time I had represented the Union abroad.

I was in no doubt about what a major responsibility I had inherited. When the members are under attack from the employer and solutions are not forthcoming, they often turn their wrath on those who are representing them, and not on the employer who is threatening them. I had seen it happen before in other areas, so it was not new. The members also believe in some cases that a change of face in their representative will bring solutions that had eluded others. I did not support that view as I knew how much effort both Charles Turnock and Frank Cannon before him had put into the grave crisis facing engineering staff. I knew that even to equal their effort, let alone reduce the threat where they had not been able to, would take a lot of hard work. That I was prepared for, and had always said that if improvements could be measured by personal effort, then we would succeed.

I knew many of the engineering reps because I had virtually been Frank Cannon's assistant in that sphere for a few years. That made my initiation easier because in the main they were dedicated rail workers and NUR members. They would support whoever was representing them through thick and thin. Loyalty like that does not exist today – or so it would appear. All the main works – Glasgow, York, Doncaster, Crewe, the Derby two and Eastleigh – were threatened, as well as Shildon.

Although I already knew Alex Ferry, the General Secretary of the Confederation of Shipbuilding and Engineering Unions, whose Unions represented about fifty per cent of BR engineering workers, I was soon to get to know him much better. Alex, being a fellow Scot, with a high reputation for dedication to his members, and I would have been expected to hit it off from the start.

It didn't begin like that at all. There was great rivalry among our respective members about their particular Union, and being a bit impetuous, and I suppose anxious to impress my own members, I felt Alex took too long to move to our next position. I am sure in retrospect he felt through his greater experience at that level than me that the old Scots maxim of 'Gang canny' was the correct strategy. We crossed swords on a number of occasions in those early days, but I am happy to say it was not long before we established a mutual respect for each other. In fact, Alex Ferry was one of the finest Trade Union Officers I had the pleasure of working with. Without being disrespectful to the Trade Unions within the Confederation, his talents were not used to their maximum benefit in the Trade Union or political field. I say that mainly because of the limited authority he had from the Unions affiliated to the Confederation, and their anxiety to retain their individual autonomy.

I pay tribute to Alex Ferry's memory, and grieve as his family must at one so talented with so much still to give on behalf of his fellow men being struck down even before he got to enjoy any of the fruits of his labour in retirement. Such is life. Well done, Alex.

The screw was really tightening on the Shildon closure; the best we were being offered was a lengthening of the final closure date by a few months, but as anyone involved in Trade Union negotiations knows this was probably built in to the original proposals.

Neil Kinnock (whom I only knew slightly) was elected Leader of the Labour Party at the 1983 Brighton Conference. A deputation from Shildon Works had been in Brighton since the start of the conference to lobby delegates about the problem, which was on the Conference agenda. They had asked for a meeting with Neil on the matter, to which he readily agreed. Alex Ferry and I accompanied Neil to the hotel, outside which the deputation had assembled on the street. I will always remember the brisk walk from the conference centre with Neil while trying to brief him on the latest position. There we were, only little more than five minutes away from the hotel, with multitudes of the press and TV at our heels. In fact Alex Ferry and I, with our national representatives, were due to meet BR Engineering Management in Brighton that day on the latest position and we already knew we were not going to alter much of the original proposals. I needn't have worried about Neil. He was brought up in the same school as me, i.e. don't tell people things they would like to hear unless they can be delivered.

I had always felt an admiration for Neil Kinnock for some time before that, and saw him as a future leader. Within a few minutes that bleak October afternoon in Brighton, I felt confident the Party had made a good choice. Neil treated me as if he had known me all his life, and in later years, when I became a member of the Labour Party National Executive, I became quite close to him. He is a good man.

The onslaught which the Tories began on all Unions in 1983 was relentless. The major manual industries had all taken it in their turn and were afterwards much weaker – particularly financially – than when they started. Yet there were still those in Executive Committees of many of the Unions, not least ours, who wanted to take the Government on. There was the enemy 'without' and the enemy 'within'. One of the troubles during my lifetime of the Trade Union and Labour Movement has been our capacity to inflict pain and suffering on ourselves. We will always fight our own more vigorously than the real enemy. The Tories must have laughed their heads off over the years.

The next lot to take a mauling was the Seamen's Union. Their opposition to cutbacks at Dover led to the full weight of the law being thrown at them. They had more than their fair share of *headbangers* in influential offices, preparing to take the Government on. They fared no better than those before them, and were heavily penalised financially, having their funds sequestrated, cars impounded, and offices closed down. We were closer to them than most Unions, as there were discussions going on about a possible merger with them, in normal circumstances. That meant we were called on to provide accommodation, transport and finance to enable them to maintain some form of activity. Because of the cost of the miners' strike and assistance to others since, the NUR finances had taken a hammering.

The Seamen came out of their dispute in a shambles as far as their financial position was concerned, which made their need for a merger very urgent indeed. Such ventures take a lot of time, however, with consultations and ballots of members over lengthy periods.

Sam McCluskie, the Seamen's General Secretary, was a very sick man and had been so for a long period. He had a serious internal cancer and most of us who knew him wondered how he had managed to survive so long.

The consultation period went on for almost two years before it was finally decided that the two Unions would merge in 1987.

In April that year Charles Turnock, the NUR Senior Assistant, retired, leaving me as the Senior Assistant; this was formally ratified by the Executive Committee. This took place before the formal merger with the Seamen.

I was very excited by my new position as principal negotiator for all British Rail staff excepting engineering staff, and in October I would be nominated for a position on the Labour Party National Executive Committee. I was into my last four years maximum before I retired and was greatly looking forward to the involvement industrially and politically.

A number of staff reorganisations were going on at BR, which

I had already been taking part in because of the impending retirement of Charlie. One which was very dear to my heart, and which I had looked forward to happening since I began work on the railway, was guards getting the opportunity of becoming drivers. Discussions about this had already been under way for about two years and although well advanced had a long way to go. There was a lot of opposition to the plan from ASLEF and a considerable amount from among the guards' reps on our EC, despite the considerable benefits which would follow. It really does become very frustrating getting progress sometimes. I often wonder if workers can ever visualise the possibility of a breakthrough after years of stagnation.

The project of guards having the opportunity to become drivers was known as the 'Traincrew Concept'. After about two years in 'Working Parties' the proposals were completed to the satisfaction of the Unions. It meant that with some initial assessment of existing guards, closely monitored by the then NUR, they would have the opportunity under the age of forty of expressing a preference to become drivers.

I had to spend a considerable time with the EC subcommittee representing guards to recommend acceptance of the proposals. It had been decided that these would be put to the guards in a ballot. By the narrowest of majorities (one) they so agreed. I had as much difficulty with our own Executive in making progress on this issue as I had with management, in fact more so because it was a management initiative.

The proposals were put to the membership early in June 1988 with the ballot closing on 28 June 1988. The result was a narrow majority in favour (384); 7,018 votes cast and 245 voting papers declared spoiled. Just as well it was not a 244 majority in favour. As they say in a democratic society, a majority of one is sufficient, and we were on our way – a major breakthrough. I think history will judge agreement on 'Traincrew Concept' to be one of the biggest membership advantages a large section of NUR members ever achieved, especially for the vast majority of them, who had no promotional future.

My only regret was that it had not been agreed in the 1960s, when 'Single Manning' was introduced. If the Unions had been bold enough it could have been achieved then. On this occasion ASLEF had been more receptive. I would like to think that may have been because of how I led for the NUR.

I was now well known among the top management of BR, having been working at Headquarters and regional level for over ten years, under the now third General Secretary. I had realised when I first became a full-time District Officer in 1966 how important it is to build working relationships with your opposite number. I always remember my old mentor, Bill Murphy (an Exeter Officer, but from Glasgow) telling me, 'When you go in to see the manager, always remember you want something from him. Because of that it is not a good idea to upend the furniture on the way in. By all means, if you don't get anything from him, there is no harm in upending it on the way out!'

I thought that was a good common-sense approach. I am sure Joe Gormley tried to teach Arthur Scargill likewise, but Arthur's learning process was slower than mine. Arthur was an 'all or nothing' man. It is very painful trying to get everything; but without care you can get nothing regularly.

I was satisfied that my approach was beneficial to those I was representing. So often at HQ level, especially regarding personal cases, they had been gone through at so many lower levels that if there had been any strength in the case it would have succeeded long before it reached us. It was in dealing with those types of claims when your relationship with your opposite number was critical. Very often it was all you had to try and succeed with, and as most of these were personal claims, it was possible to win on that basis. It was of great importance to the individual who pursued his claim, and did tremendous benefit to the Union if you succeeded. Likewise, failures on personal claims could do enormous damage to the image of the Union. News of a failure would go through the locality like wildfire, whereas success was taken for granted. I had no complaint with that; after all, that is what we were supposed to be in existence for.

During my time as an AGS from 1991, there were two National Officers below AGS. They were Brian Arundel and Wilf Proudfoot. Brian had been off on long-term sickness for some time, and Wilf had to carry on as best he could assisting us on his own. Because of the amount of time the Senior Assistant spent on Labour Party Executive work, it meant most of his time was spent assisting the Senior Assistant, or between him and the second Assistant covering the Senior. Before Charles Turnock retired, Wilf and I did a lot of work together. He was a great worker, very tenacious, and totally reliable. We got on well together. When I took over as the Senior Assistant, I was not on the Labour Party Executive, so I was able to deal with more on the negotiating side personally. I am sure Wilf welcomed the break, because he had major responsibilities on London Transport with the Engineering Workers, similar to the work I had been doing for that group with BR. Because the Union itself was going through a period of reorganisation, setting up district offices and transferring some regional and smaller company negotiations to those regional offices, it was intended to continue with two Assistants instead of three.

In normal circumstances Wilf could have expected to be elected an Assistant when Charlie retired, but it looked like he would have to wait until I retired in August 1991. Such a move was never guaranteed, although it had always prevailed in the past, until Jimmy Knapp broke the mould in 1983 by storming through on the headbangers' bandwagon. The Union was by now heavily under the influence of the 'Loony Left', so anything could happen. History will judge whether my feelings were real or imaginary. I personally have to make allowance for the 'never as good as it was' syndrome.

Trades Union Congress
L-RMT01.DBA

Congress House, Great Russell Street, London WC1B 3LS
Telephone: 071-636 4030; Fax: 071-636 0632; Telex: 268 328 TUCG

Mr A L Dodds
Senior Assistant General Secretary
National Union of Rail, Maritime and
Transport Workers
Unity House
Euston Road
London
NW1 2BL

Your reference:

If replying please quote our reference:
SIIW/PJ/TM/WP

When telephoning, please ask for:
Tom Mellish

Date:
August 1 1991

Dear Andy

HSC's Railway Industry Advisory Committee

I am writing on behalf of the TUC to congratulate and wish you well in your forthcoming retirement.

I understand that you have recently attended your last meeting of RIAC, representing the TUC.

May I take this opportunity therefore to thank you for all your hard work on RIAC. I know of the high regard with which you are held by your colleagues on that Committee. Your commitment to improving health and safety on the railways will be hard to match.

Once again congratulations on your retirement and all best wishes for the future.

Yours sincerely

Peter Jacques
Secretary
Social Insurance and
Industrial Welfare Department

General Secretary: Norman Willis
Deputy General Secretary: John Monks
Assistant General Secretaries:
Roy Jackson and David Lea, OBE

Letter of retirement from the TUC.

JH.PN

Department of Employment
Caxton House, Tothill Street, London SW1H 9NF

Telephone 01-273 5808/9
Telex 915564 Fax 01-273 5821

Parliamentary Under Secretary of State
Patrick Nicholls MP

A L Dodds Esq
2 Polperro Close
Orpington
KENT
BR2 0WB

18 November 1989

Dear Mr Dodds,

I understand that your period of office as a member of the industrial tribunals came to an end on 24 October of this year.

I should, therefore, like to thank you for your readiness to serve on the panel, and for the very valuable service you have given to the tribunals during your period of office.

Yours sincerely,

Employment Department · Training Agency
Health and Safety Executive · ACAS

Letter of retirement from the Department of Employment.

Top: personal photograph of the inside of Tutankhamun's tomb, Valley of the Kings, Egypt, March 1989.
Bottom: myself and Albert Meredith at the Pyramids of Giza, Cairo, March 1989.

From left to right, my three girls, Alison, Margaret and Phyllis.

Chapter Eight

I represented the Union on many occasions on foreign trips. They included visits to the then Soviet Union in 1983, 1990 and 1991. Foreign trips were confined to the General Secretary and his three Assistants as far as Officers were concerned, and accompanied most times by a single member of the Executive Committee. Occasionally your host would invite your wife, and on such occasions you picked up the cost of travel personally. Margaret accompanied me on visits to Stockholm and to Rome. On each trip my EC colleague was a Scot with his wife – Charles Devine in Stockholm and John Milligan with his wife in Rome.

In 1989 I was in two parts of the African continent – Egypt in March and Johannesburg in October.

In 1985 and again in 1986 I visited the former German Democratic Republic, in 1985 as guest of the GDR Railway Union and in 1986 as an observer at an International Trade Union Congress. That Congress was addressed by the then DDR President, Honecker, and President Daniel Ortega from Nicaragua.

Other visits during my ten years as an Assistant General Secretary included Stockholm, Rome, Sicily, Barcelona and Copenhagen. Every foreign visit was a great experience; most of them were made representing our Union as a fraternal delegate to our host Union's Annual Conference. We were then part of a party of international visitors, and our hosts always laid on a marvellous itinerary to ensure our visit was a memorable one. To describe them all and to do them justice would take another book. I have many souvenirs, photos and books and other memorabilia of those visits, which I now have plenty of time to reflect on.

However, there are three of my visits that I do want to record my impressions of here. The first – in fact my first trip abroad on behalf of the Union – was to the former Soviet Union in August 1983. I was accompanied by my good friends and colleagues, Tom

Ham from Derby, our then President, and Albert Meridith from the Executive Committee and Doncaster works. Albert had been on a delegation to the Soviet Union some years earlier, so he was able to brief us on some aspects of the visit. In 1983 the Communist regime was in absolute control. Who would have believed then the shambles that replaced it less than ten years later?

We flew from London to Moscow, and before leaving our office had arranged through the Foreign and Commonwealth Office for us to meet the British Ambassador in Moscow at some stage in our visit. We did not know what our itinerary was before we left, so it was not possible to make all the arrangements beforehand.

We were warmly received at the airport in Moscow by someone holding a copy of the *Railway Review*. Among the reception party was one of their interpreters whom I had met when they visited Britain. My period as host to foreign visitors to Britain between 1975 and 1981 was now coming in useful. After being greeted we were escorted to our hotel to have details of our visit explained to us. We spent that night and the next day sightseeing in Moscow. After a lavish dinner (everything was lavish as it turned out) we were to board a train for an overnight journey to Vilnius in Lithuania, on a three-deck sleeper. Here we would spend two days before a further overnight journey by train to Leningrad. At that stage of the visit that amount of information was as much as I could handle. The programme was crammed with all sorts of cultural visits.

Our hosts in Vilnius greeted us on arrival as if they had known us all their lives. They were John and Teresa, the leaders of the Union in Lithuania. Michael Lyakov, the Head of the National Union's International Section, accompanied us during the whole of our visit; I had met him before in London. We always assumed the Head was a bit more than that. I had also known his predecessor, Alexander Bovoshesky, and if he wasn't a KGB Officer I'm the proverbial Dutchman. You could not have met nicer people than they both were, helpful and friendly in every way. They were continually entertaining foreign visitors or visiting other countries themselves. We also had another member of their International Section whom I had met in London, Nicholas. To complete the party they had recruited a schoolteacher, just for this visit, another Michael. I was to meet this Michael on a later visit to Moscow in 1990.

The hospitality was overwhelming and John and Teresa were magnificent hosts. After being taken to our hotel for coffee and a short sightseeing excursion we were taken to lunch in an exclusive country restaurant. It was a feast such as I thought I had never seen before. From the lunch we went to a large railway depot, which turned out to be a total community, with all its own services, school and hospital as well. The final part of the visit was a tour of the hospital, which was well enough equipped and staffed to be able to deal with minor illnesses and accidents such as might occur in a large railway depot.

Finally the Matron of the hospital explained that she would like us to join her and some of her staff for what she described as afternoon refreshments. I never saw an afternoon tea like that – before or since! Every item of cake and fruit you could imagine, with loads of vodka, brandy and champagne to wash it down.

We left Vilnius after two very full days with our wonderful hosts, taking with us some great memories, and again travelled by overnight sleeper train to Leningrad (now St Petersburg) to continue our visit.

On arrival in Leningrad we were again greeted by the Union officials for that area, which was known as the 'October Region' of the rail system. The principal whom we spent the next two days with was named Pavlov, Russian for 'Paul', I believe. As in Vilnius, you would have thought they had known us all their life. The friendliness was overwhelming. We packed such a lot in to such a short visit – two more days, though it seemed much longer. Albert Meridith, one of my two companions, who had been on a previous visit some years earlier, was complaining mildly that there was not enough time between engagements to prepare for the next one; but he soon found that he could meet the tight deadlines with minutes to spare. Albert and Tommy Ham, our National President, my other companion, were delightful company. Both of them had previous experience of foreign visits, unlike myself, who was a novice.

The highlight of the Leningrad visit was a trip to the Petrodvorets, out on the Gulf of Finland. Hitler's forces all but destroyed it during the siege of Leningrad during the 1941–1945 war. The Soviets rebuilt it afterwards, even manufacturing fabrics identical to those destroyed by the Germans during the two-year siege. They also trained craftsmen to reproduce items of furniture that had been destroyed as well. The task must have been immense, but it was such a wonderful place it would have been a tragedy had its wonders been lost for ever.

Shortly after arriving in the Soviet Union, and learning what our programme was going to be, I had been trying to fit in a visit at some stage to the British Embassy in Moscow at a suitable time. This had been set up between our Headquarters in London and the Foreign Office, leaving me to arrange a mutually suitable date and time. As we left the hydrofoil which took us on this trip, Albert Meridith was relating one of his funny stories to our hosts (this was one of Albert's great qualities). I heard some females nearby laughing as if they might have overheard Albert and I warned him to keep them clean as the group nearby could obviously understand English. I then greeted one of the ladies of this group, enquiring if they were on holiday. She replied by saying that they worked in Moscow and then asked if I happened to be Mr Dodds. When I confirmed I was, I asked how she posed that question, and she said she was the British Ambassador's Social Secretary, and that I had been speaking to her a few days earlier arranging our forthcoming visit to the Embassy. Small world!

On the last evening of our visit to Leningrad, a Saturday night, we had been taken to a magnificent restaurant where there was a lavish floor show included. Prior to this, we were aware we were due to leave around six o'clock the next morning for a two-hour flight to a health resort called Kislovodsk, near the border of Georgia in the Caucasian Mountain region. While the festivities were in full swing, Michael, our interpreter, told me that travel itinerary for the trip to Kislovodsk had been changed. This must have been around midnight, and it didn't seem important to me. It turned out we were due to leave our hotel at 4 a.m. instead of

6 a.m. for our flight south! He assured us that despite the lateness of the hour they would ensure we would be ready to move by the appointed hour following a light breakfast they had arranged. I don't think at that time they knew the meaning of the word 'light' as far as food or drink was concerned. Even that early in the morning it was lavish; every meal included caviar and vodka and that 'light breakfast' was no exception.

It had again been a spectacular two days, in wonderful company. I often think about the people I met on that trip and what has become of them since the collapse of the Communist regime. Needless to say the two-hour flight south was a welcome respite from the rigours of the visit. Five days gone and six more to go…

We landed at a provincial airport with an English name, Mineral Waters, about an hour's journey from our destination, Kislovodsk, a spa and resort town. We were again met by our hosts from the region, led by Viktor, the Area Union Chief and stationmaster at the town station. All our hosts were among the most friendly you could ever hope to meet, and Viktor was no exception. Their kindness and comradeship was second to none. It had to be experienced to be believed. It was as if they were in competition with your hosts at the previous place. It just seemed to get better, although the first was excellent.

The highlight of the visit to this area was to be experienced on the second day when our hosts took us on a trip to Mt Elbrus, 18,481 feet high. There were chairlifts for at least half of that height, and we were taken up to that point, around 9,000 feet, in those lifts. It was a breathtaking experience, soaring above the giant pine trees for the first part of the ride.

We had left our hotel on a fairly long journey by two minibuses through beautiful countryside. We noticed on the way to the mountain that the drivers were not with us, and when we enquired as to their whereabouts, we were told we would see them as soon as we got back to the foot of the mountain. We had been picnicking on the way, and thought that was it, because their picnics are just as lavish as everything else they do. However, when we returned, a barbecue had been prepared unlike anything

I had ever seen before. Every kind of meat you could name was included, about twenty kilos for our party of about ten people, with all the liquid accompaniments to match.

I am sure two days at any one of the places on our itinerary is as much as any human being could endure.

On the morning of the day of our departure for Moscow, Viktor took us to his home to show us his model railway layout in the basement of his stationmaster's residence. It was really something, and had model locos from many countries except from the UK. Viktor gave Tommy, Albert and me a lovely beer mug from a collection he had. We learned during our visit that it was common for friends, when they gave you a gift, not to buy it, but take it from their personal belongings, as a sign of great affection. What a wonderful custom! I met the region chief later when he was here with a delegation and I sent a model of a British loco back for Viktor. Another wonderful experience.

We arrived back in Moscow to complete our visit to the Soviet Union with a meeting with the President of the Soviet Railway Workers' Union. When we arrived to see him at his Headquarters, we were told he had been called to see the Minister of Transport, who had his office in the same building.

You can imagine our astonishment, having come from Thatcher's Britain. The President was a huge man and greeted us with a hug, not unlike that commonly described as a Russian bear-hug, but he was very friendly like everyone else. We were to meet later for lunch – the usual banquet, which we were by now getting used to. I have never seen a place setting at a meal with so many different glasses for each diner, and as we were due to meet the ambassador at four o'clock that afternoon, we had a delegation meeting to decide who should stay sober. Albert and I agreed that as Tommy Ham was the President he would be in charge when we got to the embassy.

After a great social occasion, the President sent us off in his car to the embassy, where we had an excellent half-hour meeting over tea and cakes with the ambassador and some of his staff. We asked a number of questions relating to the prospect of the possibility of some trade with the Soviets in railway equipment, and while he did not have commercial staff available to answer us he said he would follow our questions up and reply to us when we returned to the UK. Less than a week after returning home we did indeed get some information relating to our questions sent to me at our Headquarters. The ambassador was very interested in our visit and received us most cordially. It was a fitting end to what had been a great experience.

Russia was certainly impressive, but the second most memorable visit I made abroad during my years as Assistant General Secretary was to South Africa in October 1988.

The former NUR had been financially assisting the South African Railway and Harbour Workers' Union for a number of years. We had hosted delegations from among their officials on a number of occasions, but they were keen to have us visit them in South Africa. I went with a member of our Executive Committee, Brian Whitehead, for five days in Johannesburg straight from the Blackpool Labour Party Conference in October 1988. The South African Union were having their Annual Delegate Conference in a hotel in Johannesburg where we were staying.

Operating as a Trade Union in the UK was becoming difficult under the Thatcher regime of that period, or so we thought; but it was a picnic compared to what our Brothers and Sisters were experiencing in South Africa. The delegates travelled for days to get there from all parts of that vast country, usually in 'old bangers' full to capacity. The conference got under way about two days late, waiting on delegates arriving.

We got a great welcome from the Union and from the delegates during our stay. It was difficult to participate in the conference because there were so many different languages used. The body language needs no interpretation though, and I felt very emotional among those proud people. If ever any race was entitled to their freedom to govern themselves, and to make mistakes, it was the South Africans. Among those whom I met, sometimes three generations of one family had only known struggle and oppression all their lives. People like me cannot even begin to imagine how oppressed they were. I had read reports and listened to those who visited us in the UK, but it was worse than anyone could even dream about.

Our movement was quite restricted and their conference was being closely observed by the police. We noticed their presence at least once, when they were making some enquiries. We did manage to visit the Union offices and meet some of the workers in the offices. We also visited COSATU (Council of South African Trade Unions) and had a discussion with the then Assistant General Secretary.

We were taken to visit a workers' hostel attached to one of the big railway depots in the outskirts of the city. Our hosts had to bribe people, including the Black South African armed guard at the entrance to the hostel, to enable our visit to take place.

I never saw such squalor in my life as I saw in that hostel. The rooms I saw had a tall single locker to keep belongings, and enough space for a single bed with a few rags for covers, and that was their lot. The few workers we saw were actually terrified to speak to us or be seen speaking to us. We really never did enough to help those proud people through the British Trade Union Movement. We merely paid lip service.

We made two trips to the infamous Soweto. The first was to see the immensity of the place, most of it a real shanty town of corrugated shacks... It was quite a long way out from the city of Johannesburg, nearly fifteen miles or so. The inhabitants travelled into the city to work by train or shared taxis. Those travelling by train clung to the sides of the trains or rode on the roof. Again, I have never seen anything like it in my life.

The second visit to Soweto was when Brian and I, who had earlier in our visit taken the Union President to a restaurant for a meal, invited him to go again. On the first occasion he was a bit nervous of being turned away, because of the apartheid policy of separating Blacks from Whites. The district where we were staying did not enforce that policy rigidly, so we were received and allowed to dine together. We had earlier indicated that if any challenge was made we would withdraw with him. When we repeated our invite, our host said he would like us to go to his home in Soweto and meet his family.

'Family' in South Africa means the whole family – parents, brothers, sisters and children, including nephews and nieces. We learned there could be as many as fourteen besides ourselves. We called at a Kentucky Fried Chicken place and took away a bucketful of chicken pieces and loads of chips, together with a few bottles of Coke. When we arrived at this small brick-built house of two small apartments, no light or toilet facilities, the whole family was gathered: father, mother, brothers, sisters and two of the President's own children and his wife. It was appalling that so many people had to share such limited space. How they managed I do not know, although there was a corrugated hut at the back of the house which I suspect was used for the overflow; it was more primitive than where I was brought up sixty years before in the miners' rows at the Southside (O'er the Water) with my four brothers and three sisters in the late 1920s and early 1930s, and until then I thought no human being could have been reared in such cramped conditions without water or toilet facilities. But here it was in the late 1980s. Before we arrived with the food, the President's young brother, who was about seventeen or eighteen, had begun his evening meal, which appeared to be a kind of watery porridge. Despite the smallness of the place and the numbers sharing it, it was spotlessly clean and tidy. I was very emotional about what I was seeing, yet helpless to do anything.

When the food was laid on the table and we all began to eat, the President's young brother began to weep openly. When I asked him what was troubling him, he told me this was the first time in his life he had sat with a white person to eat.

Who could believe that in 1988? But it was true. Can you imagine what that lad and his family must be feeling now that they are in charge of their own destiny led by their idol, Nelson Mandela?

I would love to go back to South Africa now and meet all the people who greeted me in 1988, and see the joy they must be experiencing now compared with what they were feeling like ten years ago. Their existence, as I saw during my short visit, must have been like being in prison.

Those of us who lived through the 1990s will be the envy of future generations, taking into account the transformations that took place politically throughout the world. The Communist regimes of Eastern Europe collapsed, and in the opposite direction, South Africa achieved Majority Rule.

My friends in the former Soviet Union had seemingly reached their Utopia, only now to find themselves in a society which must rank among the most corrupt in the world, after seeing their forefathers struggle to bring about a socialist society.

The transformations are so mind-boggling that it would have been difficult to make it up if you had tried, both so far as South Africa and the former Soviet Union and its allies are concerned. Having seen it so near the change is an experience never to be forgotten and will make me the envy of many in the future. I feel very privileged.

I visited Egypt in March 1989 as a guest of the Egyptian Railway Union with my colleague from the National Executive Committee, my friend Albert Meridith, who was serving his third term on the EC. We arrived in Cairo, and on this occasion it took some time before our hosts found us at the airport. However, once we met everything was fine. The customs of the country were very different to those I had experienced on foreign trips earlier. A Muslim country is not the best place for a Trade Union Official to find himself in. Still, you can get used to conforming to local customs, such as no alcohol. It is difficult but we conformed.

Most of the visit was cultural, visiting the Pyramids, the Sphinx, and so on. Being reminded that what we were seeing dated from three thousand years before Christ brought it into perspective. We were shown a ship that had only been excavated near the Pyramids in the 1950s. It was amazing. It was a large vessel, so far from the sea; it was beyond belief what the ancient kings accomplished to prepare for the afterlife. The authorities had built a special air-conditioned chamber to preserve it and to show it to the public. The Egyptians had a well-established Railway Museum which they took us to.

After a couple of days in Cairo, including a visit to Alexandria, we travelled to Luxor by overnight sleeper train. Luxor proved to be the most fascinating place I have ever visited. We went to the Valley of the Kings and went inside Tutankhamun's tomb. It was so awesome it is impossible to describe, and there were only about twelve steps down to it from the surface. By courtesy of our guides I was able to take a photograph of the inside of the tomb, which, considering I'm a novice with a camera, turned out exceedingly well. Again you had to continually remind yourself that it was five thousand years old.

Close to Luxor is the Temple of Karnak, which is another awe-inspiring sight. They conduct evening visits with a public address commentary given in various languages on various evenings. Like many other historic sites in Egypt, it makes the mind boggle at the sheer enormity of what has been built, given the fact that there were no aids available like those we know of today. I am certain I will never see anything to compare with the tombs at the Valley of the Kings or the Temple at Karnak, although temples are quite common, particularly in the area which was flooded by the creation of the Aswan Dam.

We paid a short visit to Aswan, and saw the exhibition there which explains the magnitude of the project. Again it is something to behold and not easily explained in a story of this kind. Suffice it to say, many of the historical temples and other buildings were moved piece by piece to new sites to enable them to be preserved instead of being flooded by the dam.

Most of the contents of Tutankhamun's tomb, gold and jewellery too vast to imagine, was moved from the site and is on display in the Cairo Museum. We had the opportunity of seeing that too when we returned to Cairo. One has to read about it in detail to get even a mild appreciation of such treasure, and then to realise it was only discovered in the second quarter of the twentieth century.

Our visit to Luxor and Aswan was conducted in the company of the local officials of the Railway Union, and the National President accompanied us throughout our visit. They were all delightful and friendly people, and I had the good fortune to meet some of them when they made a return visit to our country some years later.

This visit was something which I was very grateful for having had the opportunity (particularly with my friend Albert Meridith) to carry out.

Chapter Nine

At the Labour Party Conference at Blackpool in October 1987 I was elected, as expected, to the National Executive, to succeed Charles Turnock who had reached retirement age. The nice thing about my election, both for me personally and in maintaining the good image of the NUR, was that I came about third in the ballot for the twelve places allocated to the Trade Unions. Following the first meeting of the National Executive, I was allocated to all the main committees, including the Leader's (Neil Kinnock's) Campaign Committee. I was really looking forward to the next four years, confident, that although the Party lost the 1987 election, it appeared a certainty that they would win in 1992 or before then.

Neil Kinnock and the Executive had put in a tremendous amount of work since his election as Leader in 1983 to cleanse the Party of the Militant infiltration that had done so much harm. Charles Turnock had borne a lot of the unpopular workload in that area as Chairman of the Organisation Subcommittee, but Charles as an ex-commando revelled in it. He and Neil became close friends, and I was to enjoy a similar relationship with Neil shortly after election to the Executive.

Although I had still my employer responsibilities, but now only in respect of BR Staff, at least half of my time was in the political arena. A lot of the committee meetings were held in the House of Commons, and to this end I had my personal identity photograph card which enabled to come and go at the House of Commons, without having to go through the security check each time. The main work ahead was reviewing all the policies which had failed at the 1987 election and developing the fund-raising, which had grown in a big way.

This was really the big time. I was meeting constantly with those who looked destined to be in the next Government. The Tories were so disliked, particularly on account of Thatcher's arrogance, even with her own ministers, that it seemed only a matter of time. It was very exciting. There were even odd occasions when I would get a phone call at home from Neil Kinnock, wanting to consult me on some point or another. Neil knew that I would support him through thick and thin to see him gain power, and I make no apologies for that. The people in our movement I detest are those who find comfort without responsibility in opposition – Tony Benn, Dennis Skinner, Ken Livingstone and the like. They regularly opposed everything that was promoted by Neil, and showed no loyalty, even when they were soundly beaten by the vast majority in the National Executive. They would still emerge from the meeting and rubbish all the democratic decisions that had been taken to the waiting media – TV, radio and the press. There was no such thing as collective responsibility as far as they were concerned.

I had great admiration for Neil Kinnock and had seen him as a rising star in the Labour Party for some time. He was a very sincere man, but did not get the depth of support he was entitled to even from a number of his Shadow Cabinet. I told him that one day at an adjournment in an NEC meeting on the Sunday morning of the Labour Party conference when a number of them voted against an issue he wanted support for. They were then seen to be making their excuses to him in private; Robin Cook and Margaret Beckett were among them. I took Neil aside and said he ought to rid himself of them. 'Who needs enemies when you have friends like them?' I asked. He replied, saying, 'You might be right, Andy.'

In the Union, where there were usually seven or eight Communist Party members out of the twenty-four Executive Committee members, once a decision had been reached, no member of the Executive Committee would speak against that decision in public. That applied to the General Secretary, such as Sid Greene or Sid Weighell after him. It was a longstanding tradition and was rigidly observed, even by those who found it difficult. Tony Benn and his followers would not have lasted a week on the NUR Executive. The others would have crucified him the first time he spoke in public against an agreed decision.

They were pure and simple troublemakers, fellow-travellers of the Militant Tendency, always looking for an opportunity of stirring up unrest either politically or industrially.

I remember one occasion at the National Executive meeting when there was a limited rail dispute taking place. I knew from past experience that one of the three mentioned above would try to put an emergency resolution forward to escalate what was taking place. I prepared a resolution in case that happened, and sure enough, Ken Livingstone indicated to the chairman that he wanted to put an emergency resolution to the Executive on the rail dispute. He was being supported by Dennis Skinner, himself a product of the Unions, who ought to have known better. I rounded on Livingstone and indicated that as the Assistant General Secretary of the NUR I was better able than him to give an accurate account of the dispute, and as there were twelve Trade Union Officials on the National Executive, he should keep his nose out of their affairs. Neil had been out of the room when I made my contribution, but he came to me afterwards to tell me that Larry Whitty, the General Secretary, had told him how I had wiped the floor with Livingstone.

Neil couldn't stand the sight of Ken Livingstone for the same reasons as myself, and in fact I have seen Neil having to be restrained from trying to get him by the throat across the Executive table. That kind of reaction by Neil was totally out of character, but it was an indication of the negative role that Livingstone and Benn in particular played on the NEC together with Dennis Skinner. In many cases it was difficult to fall out with Dennis, because he was such a good rabble-rouser when circumstances necessitated such action. Livingstone and Skinner, although they would never admit it, were merely stooges for Tony Benn. He would make the bullets and they would fire them. As a person, Tony Benn was one of the most polite and courteous men you could wish to meet, but dangerous with it. I told him one day, 'The difference between you and me, Tony, is that you read all your socialism from books, whereas I had actually achieved mine through the poverty and inequality I had experienced all my life.'

He never tried to respond to me concerning my illustration.

I am sure they probably knew that the majority of the twelve

TU members of the NEC always met the evening before the NEC meeting to discuss the agenda, and very often either Neil himself or Roy Hattersley, his Deputy, would be in attendance to prepare us for anything major at the Executive Meeting. Nothing was left to chance, because the three mentioned above, together with one or two more, were ready to pounce at any opportunity to embarrass Neil. They never succeeded, which is why they were always ready to use the opportunities presented by the TV after – and sometimes before – the meeting to air their views publicly, again to try and undermine the authority of their leader, Neil.

Among the committees I served on in the National Executive of the Labour Party was the influential International Committee. Its budget was very limited, and although there were opportunities to represent the Party abroad, finance was always a problem. It did mean, however, that I was invited to many functions in this country when foreign socialist visits were taking place here. One regular contact in the country was with the Labour Friends of Israel, and when that country had a Labour Government, the International Committee often had an invite to lunch with the Israeli Ambassador at his home in St John's Wood. I attended several such lunches and found them to be very interesting occasions. The surroundings and the attitude of our hosts were all quite new to me and very exciting.

Another occasion which comes to mind was when Donald Anderson, the then Shadow Cabinet Foreign Secretary and one of the NUR-sponsored MPs, invited me to the House of Commons to a reception celebrating the anniversary of one of the former African colonies gaining independence.

In time I got to know Neil Kinnock very well during my four years on the National Executive, as well as the other MPs on the Executive, a number of whom were sponsored by the NUR, such as Robin Cook and Gwynneth Dunwoody. Other well-known front bench MPs sponsored by the NUR included Donald Dewar and Frank Dobson and, after the merger with the Seamen's Union, John Prescott. John was an individual I had noticed, and he appeared to me to be heading for high office in the future. They all played leading parts in the intense Policy Review Committees set up by Neil Kinnock between 1987 and 1991. I served on many of those Policy Review Bodies and therefore was in close contact with many of the leading lights on the Opposition front bench.

John Smith was also a leading member of the front bench team under Neil Kinnock, and while I did not have a close relationship with him, he was a person I admired, and we did come in contact from time to time through Neil's Campaign Committee, of which I was a member.

The Labour Party had such an abundance of brilliant Shadow Cabinet members in the last three or four years of Neil Kinnock's period of leadership that it must have been almost an embarrassment to him to know where he would place them all in government. They were so desperate to get into government, I felt certain they would become a great team. I am sure time will prove me right on this point.

One of Neil Kinnock's frontbenchers at that time not very well known to me, although I appeared to be well enough known to him, was Tony Blair. Tony was the Shadow Industry spokesman and we came together from time to time in the Policy Review Committee covering industrial law and related matters. This was a real hot potato and could make you or break you if you got it wrong. It nearly broke Barbara Castle in the Wilson Government of the 1960s. Tony Blair, who was already a rising star but had only been elected in 1979, could not afford to be promoting a policy that did not have majority support among the Trade Unions. Tony gave me the impression he had no intention of letting his political career founder this early.

One day, during the period of the Policy Review exercise, I got a phone call in my office at Euston from Tony Blair asking if I could come and meet him at the House of Commons for a chat about his draft proposals on industrial law. I arranged the meeting and found him to be a very able and comfortable person to be with. There were only the two of us in the Members' tearoom, and because of the sensitivity among the different Trade Union factions, he was keen to get an overall view of the areas in his proposals where he was likely to meet opposition and who that opposition would come from. I was already a member of his review team; each of the teams was led by a National Executive

Committee member, together with the Shadow Cabinet member with the relevant responsibility. I felt good that Tony Blair had enough confidence in my understanding of an area of such importance, to be one of the Trade Union leaders he was having a one-to-one consultation with.

It has to be remembered that this was an area where people like Arthur Scargill (who had done more than most others to bring the wrath of Thatcher down on the Trade Union Movement) was still baying about dismantling every last piece of the Thatcher legislation, whereas Neil Kinnock had made it plain he would retain much of it, particularly regarding ballots before strikes, which Scargill refused the miners in the 1983 fiasco. Neil Kinnock's views on ballots before strikes were supported by many of the Trade Union leaders, although not all of them were prepared to put their heads above the parapet to indicate that support. It was for reasons like this that Tony Blair had to be very careful as to how he proceeded. Exercises of this kind have ended the career of many a promising politician or Trade Union leader in the past...

Before I attained the post of Senior Assistant, I was a member of many national bodies in the industrial field. From about 1972 I was a member of the Industrial Tribunals, set up by the Wilson Government of the 1966 period to hear cases of unfair dismissal, sexual or racial discrimination. The Tribunal comprised an independent chairman, usually a barrister, and a Trade Union and employer's representative. They were very costly bodies to operate, having a large administrative staff, occupying buildings in the major towns and cities throughout the country. They did only the work that any well-organised Trade Union had been doing for many years, and in practice they were dealing mainly with complaints from non-Trade Union members, and from sections of industry where employers did not recognise Trade Unions. While the legislation was well meaning, in my opinion, the same effects could have been achieved by decreeing that employers must recognise Trade Unions as the vehicle for dealing with employee conditions, including wages. To maintain the freedom of the individual who did not want to be a member of the Trade Union, I would have been prepared to accept the individual's decision on that matter, as long as it was understood that is where any complaint could be dealt with, apart from that individual going to the courts on his own behalf.

That type of arrangement in my opinion would have been much better and, for the taxpayer, a lot cheaper.

Above the Tribunals, there was the Employment Appeal Panel and the full rigours of Common Law, which would consider the decisions of the original Tribunal, where a point of law was involved. The whole process was time-consuming and very costly and could have been avoided with a bit more thought by strengthening the role of Trade Unions, and making them more accountable to their members, lest that became a concern.

I remained a member of the Industrial Tribunals for about fifteen years, being reappointed after each three-year period. The appointments were made by the Ministry of Labour from recommendations the Ministry received from the TUC. Unions made the original nominations to the TUC. The employers' representatives came from nominations made to employers' organisations.

The same Wilson Government introduced Industry Training Boards, and again at various times I was a member of the Road Transport Training Board, and later the Hotels and Catering Industry Training Board. Their function was to ensure proper formal training was established in every industry. Appointment of members was through the same procedure as for Industrial Tribunals. Employers who did not provide formal training to a standard set by the Training Boards had to pay a training levy to the Training Board, who would themselves provide the training for such employers. Again there was a Levy Appeal Tribunal set up to hear appeals from employers who objected to having to pay the levy. I was a member of that Tribunal also for a number of years; its composition was quite small by comparison to the Industrial Tribunals and its workload small also. The chairman of that body was a retired very senior civil servant from the highest levels, Sir James Burnett. Because of the light workload of this panel, Sir James dealt with all the cases personally, and I sat with him a number of times. He would always say to me at the end of a case, 'I think we should have a beer now, Dodds.' He only drank halves of beer in my company, but was a very interesting man, whom I later learned had operated at the very top of the Civil Service, having been Permanent Secretary at the Ministry of Labour and the Ministry of Defence at one time.

I was also a member of a number of International Trade Union committees such as the International Food and Catering Unions and Road Transport Unions. That would usually only mean an annual meeting somewhere in Europe.

Later I was a member of a European Community Committee for Road and Rail Transport. Those were joint committees with employers, and at various times I was a member of the Road section and then the Rail section. Both were very high-powered committees, being the consultation body before EEC regulations were introduced. They usually met in Brussels or Luxembourg. It was not uncommon to have to attend those bodies on a monthly basis. I got to the stage where I could get to Brussels from Gatwick and back home as quickly as if I had been going to my office in London.

Like all organisations there are other offshoots, and if you were not careful you could become swamped in subcommittees. It suited some Trade Union reps who had a large back-up, but we in the NUR were thin on the ground and had to ensure we did not get caught up in any offshoots of the main bodies.

The Rail Transport Committee was a very influential body, and its representatives, both of employees and employers, came from among the senior ranks. I was only a member of it when I became Senior Assistant, but BR reps and those of other countries were from very senior levels. The consultation was usually with a very senior member of the Transport Commissioner's cabinet and sometimes the Commissioner himself. The work of that committee was very intense at times and extremely interesting.

Other responsibilities I had outside the normal negotiating area was as a Board Member of the National Dock Labour Board from 1983 until it was abolished some four years later. This was an appointment again made by the Ministry of Labour, and because of the NUR's connection with former British Rail Docks, where we still retained a lot of members, the Union was allocated a representative on the Board supervising dock workers' main conditions and any disputes arising. The Board usually met once a month and again comprised equal numbers of dock employers and dock employees, together with two so-called independent members. The employees, in the form of the NUR, were given the right to nominate one of those two, the other Trade Union members all being from the TGWU. The other independent member was nominated by employers.

This position was that of a company director, and the Board paid a nominal annual fee, plus an allowance for each meeting attended. The work was often very complex, because the body was set up to try and restore some order to dock work which had caused great problems throughout history because dock workers were employed on a casual basis depending on how many ships were in port at any one time. The Board certainly brought about improvements in the conditions of dock workers, who had a lot of muscle industrially as well as physically, and were not backward in using it at short notice. It was to try and eliminate the havoc that this type of action could cause which led to these measures being introduced by the Wilson Government of the 1960s. The NUR had a very respectable reputation in industry generally, as their representatives were always accepted as being well informed on their subject. I am not referring to myself in this connection, but to my predecessors, particularly my old mentor, Frank Cannon, and therefore it became a situation I had to uphold. I hope I can say I did so.

I was also a member of the British Rail Pensions Trustee Board, and the first Trade Union Chairman of the Fund's Management Committee. The BR Pension Fund was among the biggest in the country, having a portfolio of investments in excess of £7 billion. They had about five investment managing groups of merchant bankers, each managing huge parts of that portfolio. There were so many subcommittees dealing with the various matters relating to pensions and investment that it could easily have been a full-time job in itself. My time was in demand, with all the responsibilities I had, therefore I could normally only attend the odd subcommittee meeting and the main Board meetings.

It was a highly successful investment fund, mainly through

decisions taken in the 1970s to invest heavily in works of art, i.e. paintings and porcelain of international value. The decision to go into this field of investment was highly criticised at the time because pension funds had never invested in such a speculative field before, but when some of those works were sold in the late 1980s it proved to be a highly successful venture financially.

When the sale of those works of art took place, in America and Japan as well as London, hardcover catalogues were produced at a cost of around £20 for potential buyers, describing and illustrating the pieces concerned and their possible value. The prices of some were staggering, but as a Trustee of the fund I was given a copy of the catalogues, which in time I am sure will become collectors' pieces in their own right.

It was fascinating work, but one in which I could only play a minor part because of the time involved. The Trade Unions need to provide more resources to play a fuller part in this area.

Around 1984–85 The Co-operative Bank and a number of Trade Unions, one of which was the NUR, set up a Trade Union Bank known as Unity Trust Bank.

The Management Board represented all the Trade Union shareholders, such as the TGWU, the General and Municipal Union, the National and Local Government Union, the Post Office Workers' Union and the NUR. The NUR General Secretary, as with the General Secretaries of the other Unions, were directors of the bank and each of them were allowed to have a named deputy. I was the deputy for the NUR, and as such with other deputies we were an advisory body to the main Board. In practice we met a week before the directors and advised on action to be taken on the various items, thereby shortening the time they needed to spend... or lengthening the time available for them to wine and dine.

This was another string to my bow in my long list of interesting activities ancillary to those of my main function, and I am sure one wonders how anyone could find time to play a part in so many organisations. The answer to that is 'with difficulty', but I had excellent support from my Number Two at Unity House, Wilf Proudfoot. As I had done before with Frank Cannon, Wilf never refused to cover something that I asked him to do. We were a good team, again assisted by some excellent Head Office administration staff. Among those who excelled themselves in serving me were Barry Kew, Kevin Carey, Neta O'Donnell, John Wilson, and our Press Officer, Lawrie Harries. They were friends as well as colleagues.

[Author's note: Barry Kew died fighting cancer in 1992, an untimely end to a wonderful colleague, husband and father to his wife and children.]

Chapter Ten

After my appointment as Senior Assistant General Secretary in April 1987, I really had a very intense period ahead of me.

There was a lot of disappointment at the Labour Party not gaining power at the 1987 Election, but it appeared that the work of establishing complete policy changes to those that the electorate had rejected at the last two elections had to have priority, and there was going to be a lot of activity there. I was looking forward to playing a part in this and was confident that under Neil Kinnock's now established leadership it would be accomplished. If the Tories went the full term, as looked very likely because of their increasing unpopularity, I might well be retired before the next election in 1992. This prospect made me all the more keen to be part of an exercise that would result in Labour taking power shortly after my retirement, and could also provide an opportunity for me to get into one of the many quangos that would be introduced within the railway industry. John Prescott, the then Labour Shadow Transport Minister, more or less indicated there would be 'something for me to do'.

There was also considerable reorganisation taking place in our industry, as it was being prepared by the Tories for privatisation. The Union was also trying to reorganise itself, setting up district offices and internal changes to meet that new situation, together with introducing new technology within the office. I had a part to play in all those exercises, being the Officer in charge of the Union's finances, which were in a sorry state. I was also responsible for the Union's legal service to members, which was not providing assistance as efficiently as it had done in the past. This was leading to a lot of criticism from the branches, and it became obvious something drastic would have to happen to rectify this state of affairs.

Discussions were also in an advanced stage with the Seamen's Union with a prospect of a merger between us. There was a lot of work to do in this matter. The Seamen were in dire financial difficulties following their brush with the law in their recent dispute with P&O at Dover. They were dragged along that road like the Miners were by a number of militants in their midst.

Compared to the Miners and the Seamen we had so far been able to pull back from the brink on more than one occasion when the hotheads on our Executive were prepared to see the Union lose all its finances by ignoring the laws which made strikes illegal unless very stringent conditions were first met. We had been taken to court on several occasions when challenged by BR and other employers for not having met all the legal requirements. Sometimes we were given a few hours to reconsider our position when it was clear if we did not do so we would be in serious trouble. As individual officers we were all liable to have penalties applied to us, and in one such dispute a phone conversation I had had with my Kilmarnock and Hurlford branch secretary, Brian Campbell, was referred to in a legal document submitted by BR. This related to a dispute in Scotland about rolling stock being built by Barclays in Kilmarnock, while BR were closing railway workshops.

Being a Trade Union Officer in the atmosphere that existed during the period from about 1983 was like working in a minefield. You never knew whether the next step you took was going to cause a terrible explosion or not. As the years went on it got progressively worse, until nearly every decision the Union took had to be cleared by our legal advisers. It is really a wonder that we were able to continue any form of activity.

After a long period of consultation with the membership of both the NUR and the Seamen's Union and several ballots of both memberships, the decision to merge was arrived at, the effective date being 10 September 1990. There were still mountains to climb to make this decision effective, such as harmonising the different conditions and salaries being paid to staff and officers of the former Seamen's Union. They operated with full-time branch secretaries based at the major ports around the country. They couldn't be compared equally with our divisional organisers, who had much larger areas, and they covered a multitude of industries. It would be a big task and take quite a time to bring the new Union – to be known as the National Union of Rail, Maritime and Transport Workers or RMT for short – into a separate entity.

Sam McCluskie, the General Secretary of the Seamen, had for some time been suffering from a terminal illness and was unlikely to play any part in the new Union. Sam was Treasurer of the Labour Party and as such was a member of the National Executive. That in itself made history, because for the first time ever, one Union had two members of the Labour Party National Executive.

The merger, although having advantages from a membership point of view, meant that the new Union took on the liabilities as well as the assets of the Seamen. Although they had a fine Head Office and a number of residential flats in Clapham, and offices in the major ports, they had tremendous liabilities flowing from the Dover strike and the legal costs incurred. In fact, the liabilities were greater than their assets, and the NUR was itself in a poor financial state. This was mainly due to the amount of money spent on strike ballots. Branch secretaries and others were paid large sums for time off to try and ensure successful ballots. They were really milking the system, but the General Secretary did little to control the expense.

Although by the end of 1990, when the merged Unions had been established and I was moving into my last year before I would retire in July 1991, my activities did not diminish. If anything there was more to do than ever before, and little chance to begin winding down. I still enjoyed what I was doing and would not have wanted it any other way.

I spent a lot of time on Labour Party committee work and enjoyed the confidence of Neil Kinnock for doing so. Not a week went by that I did not attend at least a meeting every working day. It was all in a good cause, ensuring a Labour victory at the next election, so that it seemed worthwhile.

I went to Moscow for about two weeks in November 1990 as an observer with a number of others from British Trade Unions to the four-yearly Congress of the Communist World Federation of Trade Unions. I had also been at the previous four-yearly

Congress in East Berlin in 1986. The Communist regimes in Eastern Europe were beginning to fall apart by this time, so what I was likely to see was going to be different from what I had encountered previously.

The congress was held in the Russia Hotel overlooking the Kremlin in Moscow, and all the delegates – over one thousand from all parts of the world – were accommodated in the hotel as well. Although there was a certain amount of interest in this to those of us who were not communists, there was a great deal of sadness also. I met a number of Russians whom I had met before, either when they had been part of a delegation to our country, or in groups who had welcomed me when I led a delegation there from our Union in 1983. The signs of the system collapsing were very visible even then.

Around the hotel you could see children begging in the street. Some, themselves very young, were even looking after toddlers. I never saw anything like that in my visit in 1983. It was a very clear sign that a system which controlled everything so tightly had already broken down. The waiters serving our meals in the hotel were already dealing in anything and everything in the black market, and whereas the Soviet rouble used to be on par with the UK£ or the US$, they were now offering a different amount of roubles each mealtime for our money. It was of little use to us as all you could buy were small value souvenirs in their gift shops. Anything of value you wanted to buy had to be bought in the special 'Hard Currency' shops, because foreign currency was so much in demand.

I felt very sad for those whom I had previously met, who had genuine belief in the system that seemed to be providing for their needs and opportunities to get a good academic education, and to also be concentrating on providing first-class health care. Those were things I noticed from my earlier visit, and even making allowance for their protectiveness towards us on that earlier visit, they could not hide everything from us.

Despite the fact that the system was breaking down, there was no shortage of anything as far as we were concerned. The new President of the Soviet Rail Union laid on a dinner for the delegates and observers from Rail Unions at the congress. It was just as lavish as those I enjoyed during my earlier visit, therefore any shortages that might be being experienced had not yet reached the hierarchy of the Soviet Railway Union President.

On our way home from Moscow, we heard that Margaret Thatcher had resigned, and we thought it meant her government as well. I thought the election was about to happen. It was a false alarm.

As we now know, the Tory grandees began to see Margaret Thatcher as a threat to their reign in office. They can be quite brutal when the need arises, but to replace her with a wimp like John Major was even more astonishing, especially when it is recalled that he only entered Parliament as an MP in 1979 when she became Prime Minister. Here he was, after eleven years as an MP, having held the highest ministerial posts apart from Prime Minister, and now getting the top job. Surely this made a Labour victory even more certain than ever.

The Labour leadership certainly buckled down to complete the wide-ranging review which had been going on for several years by this time, and I was happy to play as full a part in that exercise as possible, while at the same time being fully involved in all that was going on within the Union.

Preparations would normally have been under way to elect an Assistant General Secretary to fill the vacancy there would be on my retirement in July. Vernon Hince would automatically take over as Senior Assistant, and in normal circumstances Wilf Proudfoot, the Headquarters Officer, would be the front runner in the ballot for Assistant General Secretary. Wilf was not the most popular Officer among the Hard Left on the National Executive, particularly those from London Transport, where he was the Negotiating Officer. Not being popular usually meant you were doing your job well and not allowing yourself to be a tool of the *headbangers* as I described the Hard Left.

The General Secretary was inclined to lean towards them very often, and Wilf was no favourite of his either, which may have had something to do with the election not being half in advance of a retirement as it always had been in the past.

I had been re-elected for a further year at the Labour Party Conference in October, despite the fact that I would be retiring in

July. This was quite normal and meant that although retired I would have a couple of months of retirement where I would be able to devote all of my time to work within the National Executive and I would attend the 1991 Conference as a member of the RMT delegation.

I was beginning to overlap my duties as the principal Negotiating Officer with BR with Vernon, who would take over those responsibilities when I finished, and this is where it would have been helpful if the election of an Assistant could have been completed by March 1991, and any subsequent vacancy filled as well. The whole process can take nearly a year depending on where the successful candidate comes from. Higher Officer vacancies had usually come from among the existing Officers, but there were serious moves afoot to break that mould. Ever since Jimmy Knapp had broken through the lower ranks to become General Secretary, the Hard Left – who supported him to a man – had been trying to join his team. In fact, around the time leading up to my retirement, they were at times threatening to try and remove him for not delivering to them in return for their support.

I saw a number of occasions where I thought we should be acting more quickly than we did, and where there was no division between Jimmy and myself or Vernon; but Jimmy always appeared as if he had a lot of ruffled feathers to smooth before we could move. I suppose that is part of the price you have to pay if you get into bed with the wrong people. In the atmosphere we were operating in, time was a precious commodity, and sometimes if you did not move quickly enough opportunities were lost.

The last six months before my retirement were as busy as any period since I had become an Assistant General Secretary at the end of 1981. We had always been thin on the ground at National Officer level, therefore there was no time to wind down, especially when replacements were not in place. The first four months of the year is the period when the various grades have their Annual Weekend Conference, and I was the Officer who had to deal with the now combined drivers and guards, signalmen and the supervisors and clerical section.

Before I left Moscow in November, I had a meeting with the

President of the Soviet Rail Union together with Charles Wynd, our Scottish Officer, who was at the Conference in his capacity as Chairman of the Scottish TUC. The President said he would be sending a formal invitation to us as a Union to send a delegation to the Soviet Union in the spring. He indicated that, because of my retirement coming up, he hoped that I would be part at least of the delegation.

The invitation duly arrived, and the Assistants normally took turns at leading them. In practice the General Secretary did not take part in very many foreign delegations as he often went abroad as a member of the International Transport Workers' Federation. As I had just been to the Soviet Union in November, it would have been Vernon's turn to lead the delegation planned for early May. Vernon kindly stood down so that I could go, and therefore preparations were being made for that visit. The President, John Cogger, and a member of the National Executive would make up the party. John and I had a good relationship, which is very important on trips such as this. He had never been before, whereas this would be my third visit, therefore I would be much more confident this time.

After the turn of the year in 1991, I was allowed to push forward those jobs I already had in hand, without having any new ones allocated to me.

The one that I had completed successfully over two years before, in October 1988, is that which I think was by far my greatest achievement for a section of the members, i.e. the Traincrew Concept. Guards began training as drivers almost before the ink was dry. It was a long exercise, but well worth it.

The other project that Wilf Proudfoot and I spent a lot of time on was the Permanent Way Restructuring. This would have brought major alterations to work practices for this group, albeit meaning shift working for large sections who had not experienced this type of work pattern on a regular basis, although shift working was common in the railway industry. There would have been very big movements in basic pay for almost all the existing staff, because although there would have been a scale rate of pay, all existing staff would have been on the maximum rate for their particular grade. There was a lot of opposition to the proposals, fostered by members of the Executive Committee, one of whom at least, as a machine operator, would not enjoy the huge element of overtime he had been used to getting for many years.

However, there would have been many more gainers than losers, and I had always supported distributing earnings as widely as possible. These proposals would have gone some way towards that. A higher basic pay also ranked for higher sick pay, holiday pay and eventually a higher pension. I had pushed BR a long way beyond their original offer on basic pay, and tried to persuade the Executive members to recommend it to the members. The furthest they would go was to put the proposals to the members and leave them to decide. But without a recommendation to accept, there was little chance of success.

I had to be content with a decision to put the proposals to the members in a ballot over a period of time that would at least stimulate discussion, and possibly get a decision based on the full proposals rather than on the distorted version being conveyed to the membership through some of their Executive Committee representatives. I owe a tribute to the support I received from Moray Cowan, the Permanent Way representative from Glasgow. He was under a lot of pressure from one of his Glasgow colleagues (who had opposed his every action during his term on the EC). I found Moray to be a very courageous man, not for supporting proposals which I was recommending, but for doing so in the firm belief that it would improve the conditions of the vast majority in this grade.

Although the ballot was conducted over a period of many weeks, the result was against acceptance, only 2,772 out of over 12,000 voting to accept. The overwhelming rejection appeared to be a clear message to leave things as they were. That might not have been an option, however, as management had already been introducing changes without making any payments for them. The fact that management allowed the restructuring proposals to be dropped suggests that they might have thought the price for them higher than they wanted.

In my forty-eight years of experience in the railway industry, there has always been a fascination about receiving greatly fluctuating wages from one week to the next, depending on the amount of overtime you can get. There were large sections of the network where overtime was a scarce commodity. Be that as it may, you cannot argue with democratic decisions. You have to accept that the members are not convinced at the improvements you have negotiated.

After attending a few grades conferences, such as the supervisors and the now drivers and guards, around March and April, which would be my last, I was preparing for my visit to the Soviet Union in May of 1991.

Grades conferences were always events where the members took the opportunity of grilling you and their executive representatives on policies affecting them. They had taken on a higher profile over the last few years, by having the right to have two of their successful resolutions placed on the agenda of the Annual General Meeting.

I had always enjoyed those weekend gatherings as they presented an opportunity of mixing with a large group of members who, while usually playing a part in the Union as a whole, were among the best informed regarding their own section.

As on previous occasions I was well received. The supervisors and clerical grades were always very courteous with the Senior Assistant who negotiated on their behalf. The guards' conference on the other hand was well known for giving the Senior Assistant a hard time, but with one exception in five years, I never had reason to complain.

On this, my last occasion with both of them, they marked my forthcoming retirement with presentations to me. I learned later that the guards' conference, as it had been until now, had never marked the retirement of any Officer before me with a presentation. I felt very proud that I was the one who had broken the mould.

If you leave a position with more friends than enemies, you can't have done too badly.

The time came for the trip to the Soviet Union, early in May 1991. John Cogger, the President, had been on the National

Executive twice before, and had been on foreign delegations during both those terms on the NEC, but he had never been to the Soviet Union. We were accompanied by a colleague from the NEC who was making his first trip abroad as an Executive Committee member. The practice was that EC members in their final year are those who take a turn at a trip, and the six who were on their final year nearly always got at least one trip – not always, but nearly always. The three of us were comfortable with each other, which is very important on a foreign visit.

I was particularly looking forward to the visit for a number of reasons, firstly because it would be my last before I retired in another two months; and secondly, because when I was in Moscow at the International Trade Union Conference in November 1990, I had already seen for the first time signs of our host interpreters freely criticising the government regime for failing to provide the services they had been enjoying. Although the criticism was not widespread, I noticed it as being very odd, in that people at this level were not at the bottom of the pile, and had always acted very loyally to the system. I would be taking careful note of what the situation was like this time.

As on past visits we travelled to Moscow initially, to be met by my then friends Nicholas and Michael, his chief from the Union's International Department. A visit to a youth centre had been planned for us for that evening shortly after booking in to our hotel. The arrival and clearance at the airport was later than it should have been, and Nicholas asked me if I minded if we went straight to the youth centre.

We had eaten on the plane and, although we were in need of getting freshened up, I readily agreed to fit in with his plans. This is where my experience from previous visits was valuable, because I knew that the places our hosts took us to had always been well prepared, and to keep the people waiting who were expecting us would be discourteous. When we arrived at the youth centre we were treated to the usual hospitable reception of food and drink, and an exhibition of youngsters showing us their skills in ballroom dancing. Some were very young, hardly ten years old, but they performed like adults, dressed in evening wear, with all the make-up that goes with such dress. There were older children as well, displaying Western-type dancing like rock and roll and jiving. It was a real professional display and a very entertaining way to begin our visit.

The adults in charge of the centre were very friendly and seemed pleased to have us among them. Conversation was not easy, as it all had to be done through the interpreter, but even in light-hearted discussion I could detect an uneasiness I had not noticed when I was talking with those I met before. It was not anything that my two colleagues would notice, I was sure, and I did not draw it to their attention.

After a pleasant two hours we made our way to the hotel and to get some details of our itinerary during our ten-day stay in the country. Our hotel in the centre of Moscow was as usual of a very high standard, and as the delegation leader I was usually allocated something slightly better than my colleagues. Anyone who thought that everything in the Soviet Union was of the same standard could not be more wrong. They practised a 'pecking order' system the same as we did, therefore I was seen as of higher rank than my colleagues and treated accordingly. In fact, they probably did more in this regard than we did when they visited us, because we allocated them all the same type of hotel room.

During the course of our first evening, which we were now spending in the hotel, we learned that most of our stay in the country would be spent in Kharkov, in the Ukraine. The Ukraine was one of the large industrial states, between four and five hundred miles south-west of Moscow. We spent some time the following day sightseeing in Moscow, and in the early evening prepared for an overnight sleeper train to Kharkov.

I think this is where I began to notice distinct differences from my earlier visit as a guest of the Union. This time we were to be accompanied by a female interpreter with another colleague, neither of whom I had met before. They appeared to be individuals who worked casually for the Union in this capacity, but although I had experienced this on my first visit at least one and usually two staff from the International Department had always been with us, very often the Head of the Department, Michael Lyakov. We always assumed the Head was possibly a member of the KGB as well as having his role within the Union.

Marina, our main interpreter, had clearly filled this role before, because she asked me about a colleague from the Republic of Ireland Transport Union, whom I had met in Brussels and knew. In fact I think he had come as a guest to our Annual General Meeting. Marina had visited this colleague, Michael Walsh, and his wife at their home in Ireland on at least one occasion.

John Cogger, who was a widower, developed a close relationship during our visit with Marina, and while I never kept track of it on our return, mainly because I retired shortly after, I understand Marina is now – or was – in this country on a permanent basis. If that is the case I am sure it had something to do with the altered political situation which was developing, because she was anxious not to let her friendship with John become known at that time to her bosses.

We were met at Kharkov by the District Union Officials; the boss was another female. That remark is not meant in any derogatory sense but more as a compliment, because I had met several ladies in high positions in the Union in the Soviet Union. Teresa, from Lithuania, comes to mind in that capacity. In fact, Ludmilla, our host in Kharkov, showed how pleased she was having us as her guests for the next few days by stopping our transport at a store on our way from the train to the hotel, and buying each of us a small souvenir to mark our arrival in her city.

When I refer to the Ukraine and Kharkov, one of Ukraine's major cities, as a district of the Soviet Rail Union, one has to remember the sheer size of the Soviet Union, and its being made up of so many Republics, of which the Ukraine was a very important one. Compared to our own Union in the UK, that in the Ukraine may well have been as large. The rail system in the whole of the Soviet Union was quite vast and employed millions of people.

As in Moscow we were taken to a very good class of hotel and got details of how we would spend our time in the country. It was going to be a mixture of sightseeing and visiting workplaces. The evenings were going to be spent socialising, which my colleagues and I were experts at. Our colleague from the EC was a member of the train catering grades when at work, therefore he got plenty of opportunities of practising his skills on our behalf.

We learned during a discussion with Ludmilla that her husband was a professor at the university. Some time during the course of our stay he would be joining us. It was well known that they had been practising sexual equality since the revolution. We were seeing it in practice each time we visited.

On the second day of our visit to Kharkov, Marina had engaged the services of a local tour guide to take us on a tour of the city. The guide was similar to those in cities worldwide, telling you the history of the place and pointing out all the historic buildings, etc. It was during this tour that I saw again some criticism of the regime by this young man. Something official was taking place in the city while he was explaining the surroundings to us. The event which was taking place caused him to stop his commentary briefly, and he did not hide his impatience at this from us. He was quite openly critical. This would never have occurred in the past, but I saw it as a development of what I had spotted happening among those around us in Moscow in November 1990.

We spent a pleasant few days in Kharkov and eventually did get to meet Ludmilla's husband at one of the many social events that took place in the evening. He was a charming man and, like myself, a pipe smoker. It is amazing how something like that can make you at ease with people sooner than you might do otherwise. He was very proud of his wife's position within the Railway Union.

We met other Union colleagues during our stay and a number of workers at places we visited. We did not get into details at any stage about the worsening political situation, as it would have been discourteous to do that, but I kept watching for signs that I had seen in Moscow. However, I have to say that, with the exception of the instance with the tour guide, I did not detect any uneasiness.

We began our journey back to Moscow, having spent four days in Kharkov among people offering us so much warmth and sincerity.

We again travelled by overnight train, in two-berth sleeping compartments, unlike the sandwich of three-berth ones we travelled on during my first visit to the Soviet Union. The trains were clean and comfortable, but were not spectacular in any way when compared with our own. Any food or drink we had was what was carried with us. Nevertheless, rail has always been my favourite form of travel, because you see all the countryside as you go. That always interests me, particularly in a foreign country. Sleeping did not come easily to me, and therefore I was up as soon as it was light enough to see the countryside.

From the number of long stops we were having it became obvious that there was something seriously wrong, but as was the case with British Rail, if you are a passenger it is very difficult to get any information when delay is occurring. I found from my earlier visit that the people around us did not appear to like or be able to answer questions about things that were not going smoothly. I never found out whether they look upon these kinds of situations as a failure of their system or not.

It was only after we arrived in Moscow after a journey lasting about fourteen hours, which shouldn't have taken more than ten hours at the outside, that we learned that there had been a very bad disruption of the service on our route due to a derailment of a train and that our train had to be diverted. Nothing wrong with that; it happens all the time on British Rail. Despite the length of time we spent on that train I enjoyed the experience because, unlike flying, you are seeing something new all the time the train is travelling. The one noticeable thing about that journey, and indeed those I made by train on my first visit, was that there was no shortage of staff to look after the passengers' welfare. They certainly had their priorities right in that area.

When we arrived back in Moscow we still had about three days of our visit left. Arrangements were in hand to take us on a visit to the city of Yaroslavl, about two hundred miles north-east of Moscow. I felt by this time, after nearly a week in the Soviet Union, that our visit was a rather lacklustre affair compared to my first visit to the Union in 1983. Maybe it was because of the rapidly changing political situation. That must by then have been a very serious matter internally in the Soviet Union. We were not meeting people like the groups of workers' representatives we had met previously in railway depots, etc. I am certain there was no intention of making us feel uncomfortable, but it was apparent that the people at the head of the Union, who had previously been very influential and close to the power base in the Government, were now very much preoccupied with other matters. Maybe in view of the rapidly changing situation it is a wonder the visit took place at all.

Be all that as it may, the visit continued. Under Marina's guidance we travelled to Yaroslavl, which we learned was one of the very few religious cities in the Soviet Union. There were many fine religious buildings to see, one in particular which appeared to be the equivalent of one of our fine cathedrals. There was also a very 'high' solemn service taking place during our visit, with lots of religious leaders in very colourful vestments of great elegance. Among them was one dressed even more elaborately than the others whom I took to be the equal of at least a bishop or maybe even an archbishop. This was an unusual scene in the Soviet Union, and although I had been shown a church when I visited Lithuania in 1983, more by accident than design, this visit had been specially organised. It was a very interesting occasion, and certainly differed from railway establishments! Yet I found the whole visit a bit of an anticlimax compared to my first visit. I suppose because it was all new to me then everything seemed overwhelming.

We returned from Yaroslavl to Moscow to spend one more day there before returning to London.

It is always on the final day, apparently, that you get to meet the President of the Union, and so it was on this occasion. This took place at the Union Headquarters, where we were met by the President and a number of his colleagues. With the exception of himself and Michael Lyakov, Head of the International Department, and his colleague, Nicholas, there was no one that I had met before. We discussed some general matters, as we had always done, and they emphasised how importantly the need to maintain world peace was. This had always been one of their high priorities. I always believed those who expressed views of that nature to me were very sincere about it. I am not so sure I would give their leaders in the past the same support, bearing in mind their incursions into other countries since the end of the Second World War. Gorbachev appeared to be ploughing a different furrow, but he was already in big trouble.

I tried gently to get some discussion on the internal political situation, especially because of the obvious changes that were showing; even at that time Yeltsin's name was cropping up regularly, whereas it seemed like only a short time before that he had been a joke figure in the Soviet Union, and portrayed as a drunk. Maybe it was the propaganda machine at work which was conveying that image. Needless to say, our hosts kept their views on internal matters close to their chests.

We were treated to a very impressive farewell lunch following our discussion. Whatever other changes were taking place, their generosity and friendship did not change towards their guests.

Chapter Eleven

When I returned from my visit to the Soviet Union there was only another two months to go before I would be retired. The main event in that time would be the Annual General Meeting, due to be held in Ayr at the end of June. I had not given a lot of thought to how I would cope with not having to go to work every day. I suppose it would take some time to adjust after having been employed continuously since I left school at fourteen years of age – some fifty-one years in all. There was so much happening you did not get much time to think about the future.

I did feel that there wasn't a lot of evidence of great improvements in the industry since I had come into it forty-eight years earlier. That made me very sad, particularly because I felt we as a Union could have done a lot more than we did to bring about greater improvements.

My Union had moved from being one of the most affluent to becoming one of the worst off as far as its finances were concerned inside the last ten years. Operating under the Thatcher regime was very expensive and much more time-consuming than it had been in the past. Legislation directed at the Trade Unions was intended to do exactly that, but we made decisions that added to our costs that we never should have. Provision was made in the Trade Union legislation to recover costs of ballots, but the TUC would not allow affiliated Unions to take advantage of this. Yet even when they eased that position, the then NUR Executive and members, through the Annual General Meeting, would not agree to make applications to the Government for reimbursement of expenditure in that area. We were continually conducting ballots for industrial action in one part of the industry or another over a long period. That was our job – protecting and improving members' pay and conditions – but we could have done it more effectively and less expensively on many occasions.

The internal reorganisation that we knew needed to be carried out to make the Union efficient and cost-effective was being hampered by staff and the Executive Committee at every turn. The Executive Committee resisted any attempt at cost-cutting which had a direct effect on them. It was becoming a futile exercise, and although some economies were being made they were only tinkering with a major problem.

I had been given the task from the General Secretary of trying to reorganise the Head Office legal department, which had become inefficient as well as expensive to run. I told the General Secretary that in my opinion the only solution was to virtually close the department, letting the solicitors take over their function from the outset in any legal involvement of members. Eventually they did this in any case, but only after a time lapse when the department tried to reach settlements. There was a lot of resistance from the staff to this proposal, even though they were guaranteed that nobody would be dispensed with as a result. It was the old case of Parkinson's law taking place. Despite the opposition, and with the help of the Unions' solicitors in Scotland, McPhail and Co., and Pattinson and Brewer in England, the plan was put into effect. They would benefit financially by increased activity, but eliminating a department, staffed by around twelve people and costing around £500,000 annually, would be more economic and from the members' point of view more efficient, especially in bringing about earlier settlements.

This was a step that ought to have been taken twenty years earlier, but in those days there was little need, it seemed, to effect economies. The Union had always been financially sound, or so it appeared. The fact is that the members were paying for the Union's inefficiency.

As a Union looking after the members' problems at the workplace we appeared to be fairly good. Running the Union as a business, with a huge cash turnover, we were worse than a corner sweet shop. However far back you looked, nobody had the responsibility for running it as a business. I am sure I was not the first among Officers in the past to have come to this conclusion, but it was not a popular road to set out on. In the past, Officers at my level did not have to be re-elected periodically, therefore it makes you wonder why they did not pick up this problem before now. Maybe they preferred a quiet life.

I had to convince the General Secretary to let me take the proposals forward on the basis that I was soon to retire, and if I got the proposals past the point of no return, then he could take the credit when the benefits accrued. Jimmy did not like the idea of doing things that caused him short-term problems, as this would, but to his credit he saw the need for it and it went ahead. I am sure he and the Union (the members) are better served than they were hitherto in this area.

Other proposals to effect meaningful economies, as I stated earlier, were more difficult to bring about. This was because the next huge expenditure was the cost of the Executive Committee. There were twenty-four of them, full time, at a cost of around £750,000 annually. With a different form of working, such as the Negotiating Committee, comprising one third of their number, being full time, the cost could be almost halved. My old colleague, Charles Turnock, described that scenario as like asking turkeys to vote for an early Xmas. It would take a long time to bring about a reduction in that area.

On our way to the AGM at Ayr in June, I had been invited to a small social function that Leeds City branch had arranged to mark my retirement, thanks to Sandy Hamilton. He was one of the many stalwarts who served the Union at local level. I had always enjoyed good relations with Sandy and his branch as I did with most branches. My visit on this occasion involved being introduced to members around the city at their work, and also meeting local managers. This was a function I enjoyed – flying the flag as it were. It was always a great moral booster to local members for one of their Officers to be seen meeting them at work. I had always advocated that we ought to have done a lot more of it. There was a real enthusiastic bunch of local officials in Leeds City branch, led by Sandy and one of his Brothers who was on the Permanent Way Staff and a Sectional Council Representative. They were the real salt of the earth, the backbone of the Union.

Later they entertained Margaret and me at a social evening where we were made a presentation of an electric slow cooker, together with a beautiful floral arrangement for Margaret. Margaret was always well received on such occasions and had been a great support to me in my thirty-one years with the Union (more about that later). It was really nice to receive the kind of appreciation which I received in Leeds on my approach to retirement. I had always felt that if the members see that you are trying to ease their lot, even though many times it is not possible, they will respect you for the effort. I had made that my benchmark from the time I started working for the Union as an Administration Officer back in 1960. I am sure it was through that type of approach that got me first recognised when I sought election in 1966 as a Divisional Officer. It had stood me in good stead all those years. What a nice way to end your period in a job which was to help others.

I eventually arrived in Ayr for a couple of days of preliminary discussions with the General Secretary and with Vernon Hince, my other Assistant colleague. This was a usual session prior to the meeting of the Union's governing body, the Annual General Meeting. This would be my tenth AGM since election as an Assistant in 1981, although I had previously attended one as an Acting Assistant, also in Ayr, around 1976.

Our discussions were aimed at allocating the items each of us would deal with and also at deciding the approach to major items affecting existing policy. I was looking forward to my final AGM being held in the area where I had began as a Union member forty-eight years earlier in 1943. I had been a very active local member in the late 1940s and early 1950s and was well known in the area. I was sure this would be a fitting finale.

Ayr had always been a popular venue for our Union at national or grade level to have annual conferences. The hospitality of the branch was overwhelming on such occasions, and led to conferences coming back time and again. The year 1991 was to be no exception, and most of it was laid on for my benefit. I was still having to perform, as far as the agenda was concerned, and nobody let you off lightly just because you were about to retire, and neither should they have. This was the delegates' big day and they had to convey to those who elected them that they were worthy of that decision, by vigorously pursuing the items from their district. I would not have wanted to see it any other way.

Each evening after the day's business there was a different social function to attend, every one proving to be better (if that was possible) than the last one. You had to have great stamina to keep pace with all that was taking place. I had had good practice after all those years and appeared to be coping.

My three sisters from Muirkirk, Maisie, Anna and Betty, together with George, Anna's husband, and Jack, Betty's husband, were able to join in one or two of the social evenings, as were one or two of my local friends from the old days. It soon became quite an emotional occasion, as I should have known it would be, because although they were mainly social evenings there was usually a short time allowed for some remarks to be made. It was then that Margaret and I were in the midst of things.

Presentations were made to me and Margaret by John Milligan on behalf of Conference through a collection among the delegates of matching gold wristwatches, suitably inscribed to mark the occasion. I was thrilled, particularly as Margaret's contribution to my work was again being acknowledged. The Ayr branch also made a presentation to me of a beautiful framed picture showing a view of Ayr.

Although the ScotRail management team came to Ayr to entertain the Officers and their partners to dinner, which again was normal at Annual General Meetings, Cyril Bleasedale, the Managing Director in Scotland, and his Personnel Manager, Hugh Watson, invited Margaret and me to a special retirement dinner in a luxury hotel in Glasgow as well. I had often represented the Union at negotiating meetings in Scotland over the last ten years, and they said this was their way of saying goodbye to me. I was presented with a beautiful inscribed crystal ship's decanter, and the usual bottle of good 'hard stuff' to fill it. I was made to feel very proud, and again Margaret was not forgotten, getting a lovely bouquet of flowers.

I loved my job very much, and to get recognition for what

people seemed to think had been done well was something that made me very humble, because I was fortunate to have had the opportunity.

Ayr certainly began the final countdown to my retirement. I could not have organised a more fitting setting for that to happen. It was a wonderful feeling after all those years to have reached the level in the Union I had. Nothing that had happened in the thirty-one years since I began working for the Union had been planned following that first appointment. If I had planned it all I might have made it to the top as General Secretary. There is no doubt that between Jimmy Knapp and me in the 1983 election, I was the one with the experience. Trade Union elections, like political elections, don't always produce the most qualified person. It is a business full of intrigue and deceit, which was not my style. Maybe having a clear conscience is better than getting to the top.

It was now time for heading south from Ayr, primarily to clear my desk for my departure on 12 July.

Two more social functions took place in the last few weeks. The first was organised by the staff at Unity House, where I had begun my career with the Union in 1960. I had studied shorthand and typing then, gaining an RSA certificate and thereby promotion. I spent six and a half years as a member of the administration staff, and when I was elected as a Divisional Officer in 1966, I was the second person only from the staff to have been elected an Officer. From that point of view, I had opened up an avenue for others in the future. Most of the staff, certainly those at my level, looked upon me with some pride as being 'one of them'. I was very pleased to have made the breakthrough that I had done, and for the recognition of it from my colleagues on the administration in the form of this function and the crystal clock they presented me with to mark the occasion. Tom Sawyer, then Labour Party Chairman (now the General Secretary of the party), came to this function.

My real 'finale' was the Retirement Dinner organised at Charing Cross Hotel by the Union on my behalf. Colleagues from ASLEF, TSSA and my good friend, Alex Ferry, General Secretary of the Confederation of Shipbuilding and Engineering

Unions, were present. Alex and I shared the office of Joint Secretary of the Railway Shopmen's National Council for several years.

I suppose Neil Kinnock's attendance was one of the highlights of this final occasion, and the remarks by Neil and the General Secretary, Jimmy Knapp, cannot be better described than by the article which subsequently appeared in the *Transport Review* of 30 August 1991.

The special point for me, of course, was the fact that my family were at this function: Margaret, Phyllis and Alison – 'my three girls' as I was proud to call them. They had sacrificed so much to enable me to pursue my career, with very little complaint. Laurence and Keith, husbands of Phyllis and Alison, were also present.

There was another session of presentations from colleagues in the other Unions, and the one I had specially requested from my own Union, a set of golf clubs, to let me try my skills at something I had taken a great liking to. To me this would be put to better use than the usual clock often presented for you to watch! At the end of all the festivities, which had been going on for over six months, I catalogued all the retirement presents, which totalled in excess of thirty gifts, ranging from cameras, clocks to watches, a television set and a music centre; and someone even suggested work by making a gift of a lawnmower – albeit an electric one!

This was it, then. I had reached the end of a journey I began in 1943 when I started work on the railway. I only wished I could do it all again.

Postscript

I wish I could wrap this part of my autobiography up in a few pages by recording that everything went according to plan and that Margaret and I spent several years travelling the world. We all know life is rarely like that, except in Mills and Boon where the characters all live 'happily ever after'.

First of all I want to say how much I owe to my three girls for helping me through my career. Without them I could not have done it. Margaret, particularly, got the heavy end of the stick a lot of the time. I am sure now, and yes, even at the time, that some of my actions caused her great pain. For those occasions, Margaret, I am truly sorry. I hope to make it up to you for your support. You have been wonderful, and I love you for everything.

To my other two girls, Phyllis and Alison, I have to say how proud they both have made me. They provided Margaret and me with a grandson and granddaughter each. What more could you ask for? I often put the Union's work ahead of their needs in their younger life, but they seemed so much a part of it all my life. When I used to say to Alison that something or other that she wanted to do was difficult for me because I was going to the Labour Party, she could not understand why I couldn't take her to the 'party'! Both Phyllis and Alison grew up with me always being involved in Trade Union and political affairs. They helped run committee rooms at local and general elections from a very early age. They were wonderful girls (Alison still is) and made me very proud of them. There's many a scrape they got me out of... Thank you for everything, Phyllis and Alison.

Within weeks of my retiring Margaret and I were shattered by the news that Phyllis had been having examinations for possible breast cancer. The early tests proved positive, resulting in a partial mastectomy, followed by chemotherapy and radiation treatment. If the original cancer is not a killer, then one of the two treatments will almost certainly bring the end. In Phyllis's case she developed leukaemia, which required a bone marrow transplant. At the end of 1992, Alison was found to be an identical match to Phyllis for the purposes of the transplant, but she was five months pregnant. The hospital decided to take the donated marrow then and freeze it until Phyllis was ready to receive it at the end of January 1993. There was considerable risk to Alison and her unborn child in making the donation, but it goes without saying there was no hesitation.

I only wish I could say it was all successful, but in fact it was not. I cannot describe the pain and suffering Phyllis went through to try and beat the cancer scourge. Alison's child, Esther, was born on 28 April, and Phyllis, who had been struggling for some time, seemed to have been hanging on for Esther to arrive. Phyllis died on 9 May 1993, after fighting so bravely to survive.

Even the arrival of Esther could only dull the pain caused by the loss of Phyllis. It was indeed proving to be a cruel world. Here was a girl not yet forty, who had earlier lost a husband when she was twenty-eight years old, having her life taken as well. We thought she had paid the price of a decent life when John died, by fighting back from that tragedy to give birth to her two children from her marriage to Laurence.

We all love you, Phyllis.